Africa and the Caribbean

AFRICA AND THE CARIBBEAN

THE LEGACIES OF A LINK

EDITED BY MARGARET E. CRAHAN
AND FRANKLIN W. KNIGHT

THE JOHNS HOPKINS UNIVERSITY PRESS
BALTIMORE AND LONDON

This book has been brought to publication with the generous assistance of the Andrew W. Mellon Foundation.

Manufactured in the United States of America

The Johns Hopkins University Press, Baltimore, Maryland 21218
The Johns Hopkins Press Ltd., London

Library of Congress Catalog Number 78-20531
ISBN 0-8018-2186-X

Library of Congress Cataloging in Publication data will be found on the last printed page of this book.

CONTENTS

PREFACE

The original motivation for this volume springs from our mutual preoccupation with communicating the variety and complexity of the African heritage throughout the Caribbean. The more we thought, taught, and did research on Caribbean themes, the deeper became our fascination with the contributions of Africa to the polyglot culture of the region as well as the erratic modifications imposed by the special circumstances of Caribbean history on the Afro-Caribbean society. The confluence of a variety of African cultures, plus the consistent input of European and local Amerindian elements, produced through the centuries a striking amalgam of linguistic, religious, dietary, familial, literary, and artistic currents that resulted in a uniquely rich, diverse, and dynamic Afro-Caribbean culture. Such a culture was neither static nor homogenous across the Caribbean. Rather, the peculiar history of regional colonialism, imperialism, and the ebb and flow of the transatlantic slave trade produced the individual variations on a common theme. By the late sixteenth century the development of an Afro-American culture was an inescapable fact of Caribbean existence.

Given the complex, multilayered, and polyphonic nature of Caribbean culture, any analysis of the region requires *ab initio* both an interdisciplinary and a multidisciplinary approach. This need has characterized the best writing on the Caribbean and has been eloquently advocated by such scholars as Arturo Morales Carrión and William A. Green. Nevertheless, the degree of interchange among the academic disciplines can be strengthened, and in some cases the reciprocal associations still need to be established. The conscious aim of the authors of the essays in this volume is to reach out from the firm ground of their formal disciplines and open their special interests in a way that appeals to specialists and nonspecialists alike. We think this awareness and this approach constitute a viable attempt at a collection of essays that is both interdisciplinary and multidisciplinary. We can think of no other way to ponder, with greater expectation of efficacy, the variegated dilemma of the African heritage in the Caribbean.

The theme of the African legacy of Caribbean societies could never be exhausted by any one book, nor in any one discussion, however long. Nor have we tried to achieve a comprehensive coverage of themes or disciplines. We think that these essays represent sufficient span to illustrate adequately the importance and the broad ramifications of a general subject previously underrepresented in the available literature on the Caribbean. We point out in the first chapter that themes dealing with African slavery and the transatlantic slave trade dominate the considerations of African influence on Caribbean society. Certain aspects formerly deemed exotic or esoteric—such as *vodun* in Haiti, and *santería* in Cuba, Trinidad, and elsewhere—have also attracted great interest. By contrast, sociolinguistic research of the type exemplified in this collection by Maureen Warner Lewis is extremely rare, with possibly less than six qualified persons currently engaged in such research. Equally surprising is the fact that the opportunities for pursuing this type of research are fast disappearing throughout the Caribbean due to political and social changes. Rare, too, is the particular perspective that Monica Schuler brings to her study of Myalism. For, as she correctly points out, merely to review popular sectarianism such as Myalism within the context of the other manifestations of lower-class escapism and anticolonialism is both too narrow and too inadequate. Their social relevance and cultural importance as a religion can only be fully understood when placed in the broader context of African folk and religious traditions. From this perspective Schuler's study certainly makes great sense not only for Jamaica but also for the entire Caribbean. It therefore provides a basis for looking at the entire gamut of African religious phenomena across the region. Indeed, Myalism in Jamaica seems to provide patent parallels with *santería* as practiced in Cuba and Trinidad—Puerto Rican *santería* seems to be a recent derivative of the Cuban model—probably because they all hold obvious concepts germane to the Yoruba beliefs of southwestern Nigeria.

One minor disappointment affected our original plans and is reflected in the collection. We thought—hoped is, perhaps, a more accurate word—that it would have been possible to include more scholars with pan-Caribbean interests. This would have resulted in the inclusion of a greater number of papers that cross national territorial and linguistic boundaries. Such an organically integrated treatment would, ideally, simultaneously reflect the common general patterns of African influences in the Caribbean as well as the individual variations manifest from place to place. Except in the field of contemporary politics, however, very few scholars specialize in broad pan-

Caribbean themes. Only the first two chapters addressed the region as a whole. We remain sadly aware that the era of continued accumulation of parallel studies and only modified insularity is far from over. There is room for hope, however. Already the disciplinary fields are intermingling and broadening their traditional approaches. That is a most welcome development that might soon spread beyond the halls of academe. Moreover, this tendency stands to derive further impetus from some of the new regional scholarly organizations, such as the *Centro de Estudios Avanzados de Puerto Rico y El Caribe* and the Association of Caribbean University and Research Institutions (ACURIL). Above all, pessimism about imminent political and economic union ought not to inhibit scholarly cooperation and collaboration.

We are convinced of the merit of the multidisciplinary approach reflected in this volume and believe that the price paid in lack of coherence remains modest. Imposing a common approach or a uniform *modus operandi* promised greater facility and efficacy under different circumstances. The editorial chores, too, would have been considerably lighter. But the trade-off would have been damaging. The complete volume would almost inevitably have betrayed a historical bias at worst—and a general social science bias at best. In either case the result would have been uncomfortably myopic. Our goal of delineating and understanding the impact of Africa on Caribbean societies is much better served by including, insofar as was possible, the greatest range and variety of disciplines and approaches. Having therefore diligently solicited the support of those whom we consider to be in the forefront of their respective fields, we set only the most minor limitations on their work.

This collection also broadly illustrates the breadth and quality of the research currently being conducted in various fields of Caribbean scholarship. It demonstrates, implicitly and explicitly, some changes that are taking place in theory and methodology. New questions are being asked, and even the old questions are being reformulated. As such, the research from which these examples are drawn increases not only our understanding of the Caribbean but also our capacity to do fruitful research on other multiethnic and pluralistic societies of the Atlantic world.

In many ways, the issue of slavery best illustrates the recent changes in Caribbean historiography. One way or another, with varying degrees of involvement, the problems of slavery impinge on every chapter of this book. Yet the assumptions of our authors vary enormously from those of previous generations of scholars, especially those prior to 1940. Slavery, of course, is one of the inescapable forces of Caribbean life and history. But the traditional concept of the history of slavery was usually a very simple and simplistic chronological narrative, which, at its least sophisticated level, managed to strip slaves, Africans and Afro-Americans, of every sense and sensibility and to reduce Caribbean history to two historical epochs divided by emancipation. Narrations of slavery, emancipation, and postemancipation replaced the unavoidable lack of other conventional political indicators of the European metropolitan countries such as dynastic changes, parliamentary dissolutions, and wars. Fortunately, the realities of the Caribbean made such continued imitation absurd. Nevertheless, for far too long, whether from an extra-Caribbean or an intra-Caribbean focus, too many works overemphasized the two-dimensional nature of slaves and former slaves. With some exceptions, the writings fell into two narrow categories of either history or folklore. The few exceptions, however, were important and influential in the historiography.

Fernando Ortiz, Lydia Cabrera, and Nicolás Guillén from the early decades of the twentieth century pioneered the views that Africans were more than impassive slaves, and their contribution to the formation of Caribbean society more than units of labor and abstract categories for statistical compilation. Eric Williams, C.L.R. James, Ramiro Guerra y Sánchez, and Lowell Ragatz explored the economic motives for the structural changes in the area, and their theories greatly discomfited the upholders of the traditional views of how change occurred in the Caribbean. After the Second World War, a whole new generation emerged and their influence remains strong today. Philip Curtin, Elsa Goveia, Gabriel Debien, and Manuel Moreno Fraginals—to be selective, rather than comprehensive—all described a Caribbean community and society, complex, interrelated, and generating its own peculiar internal logic, customs, appeals, and loyalties. The multidisciplinary span of these writers effectively removed the prevailing intellectual limitations and established new paths along which other scholars could make enormous progress. That is why the common underlying assumptions of all the authors included in this volume seem so uniform on the subject of slavery. All accept the entire issue of slavery as merely one facet of more complex social relationships in the process of cultural evolution. The first two chapters treat the transatlantic slave trade as a migration of people, and the reality of slavery as a form of culture transfer, reconstitution, and creation. To a greater or lesser extent this understanding is shared by other contributors.

Africa and the Caribbean: The Legacies of a Link is a collection of essays that explores the impact that the connection and the heritage of Africa had, and continues to have, on the societies of the Caribbean island states. These seven essays and eight authors represent five main academic disciplines. Margaret Crahan, Barry Higman, Franklin Knight, and Monica Schuler are historians. Harry Hoetink is a sociologist. Judith Bettelheim is an art historian. Maureen Warner Lewis is a sociolinguist. Lorna Williams is a literary critic. Here, however, their formal disciplinary boundaries are not stressed. Rather, they have all tried to speak with a common language to a common audience.

The first two chapters provide the regional overview, tracing the complex genesis of Caribbean societies. Knight and Crahan illustrate both the parallels as well as the contrasts in the patterns of demographic growth, migrant streams, socioeconomic infrastructures; and the consequential constraints on the process of cultural formation. Hoetink focuses on the sociological influences of Caribbean community formation, establishing three principal types of cultural influences on regional community formation, which ultimately gave a distinctiveness to the area. These he defines as anthroculture, socioculture, and ethnic group boundary.

In chapter 3 Barry Higman analyses African and Creole family patterns in Trinidad in 1813. After a brief background history of the island, he compares Trinidad with the other English Caribbean islands as well as with the United States of America. The data for Trinidad are extremely rich and provide invaluable insights into the demographic structure of the slave society in the New World in its final phase of disintegration. His sophisticated and perceptive elaboration of the contrasts between African and Afro-American mating habits, reproductive rates, and family conduct has no equivalent in the current historical literature. It is a solid basis for further enquiry into the development of contemporary Afro-Caribbean family patterns.

Monica Schuler's examination of Myalism in chapter 4 is perhaps the best available synthesis of the syncretic nature of Afro-Jamaican religious traditions. She emphatically articulates the view that the symbolic value of these religious cults has been considerably underestimated by historians. Myalism and the other forms of popular Afro-Caribbean religious movements played a tremendous role in helping the masses cope with the difficulties of their daily lives by channeling their protests against the exacting conditions of survival as well as operating as a major centripetal force on their communities.

The main concern of Judith Bettelheim in chapter 5 is to trace the origins and the diffusion of artistic components of African folk festivals throughout the islands and on some of the mainland enclaves. She finds Jonkonnu not only eclectic but particularly susceptible to varying political and social influences. Bettelheim suggests that her observations may be applicable to a wide variety of Afro-Caribbean folk art.

In chapter 6 Maureen Warner Lewis displays rare technical competence in her fascinating discussion of the African impact on languages and literature in the English-speaking Caribbean. Based on extensive field work in Trinidad, Jamaica, and Nigeria, she has identified and analyzed lexical and syntactic elements of Yoruba, Kikongo, Hausa, Fon, Arabic, Nago, Mahi, and Twi languages in the West Indies. By referring to a variety of spoken as well as written examples of Caribbean speech and literature, she clarifies the enormous impact of the African heritage on contemporary speech patterns and illuminates the symbiotic relationship between African, East Indian, and European languages and cultures in the Caribbean context.

In chapter 7 Lorna Williams examines the African presence in the poetic imagery and ideas of the Cuban, Nicolás Guillén, the most universally acclaimed of Caribbean poets. Guillén's broad scope and prolific pen allow our critic to use his poetry as the basis for exploring the various, often contradictory, images of Africa in the Caribbean consciousness. This Antillean consciousness is shaped by the racial and linguistic legacy and nurtured by the kaleidoscopic political exigencies of our times such as the Mau Mau events of Kenya, the Rastafari movement of Jamaica, and the Cuban military and humanistic involvement in many states of the African continent. Guillén sees Africa as past, present, and future. In his poetry, Africa is more than just a legacy; and its appeal transcends the ideological concerns of *nègritude*. Africa is the integral link in the fraternal chain that unites all the oppressed and exploited nations of the world. Neither Guillén nor Williams go so far as to proclaim that Africa is the alpha and omega of Caribbean existence, but the reader almost gets an impression that we have come full circle from the initial demographic and cultural impact to the current political and intellectual preoccupations. In a sense, this is a marvelously pertinent dimension of the African legacy, and one could hardly find a better expression for this idea than in the person and poetry of Guillen. As Williams elaborates, Guillen is not merely a poet: he is a political and popular poet, advocating the independence of Africa along with the defeat and destruction of capitalism, colonialism, and imperialism. His poetry is flavored with sounds and symbols in which past, present, and future meet, mix, dissolve, and often become confused and confusing. One thread, however, remains constant: the profound admiration for the African past and the unswerving faith that the diversity of the Caribbean can be an asset in its social development.

The sequential order in which we acknowledge our gratitude does not reflect the relative merit of the assistance rendered by the individuals and institutions named. All our contributing authors were unfailingly encouraging, understanding, and courteous, and we thank them for making our work so pleasant. During the academic year 1977/78 Margaret E. Crahan was the John Courtney Murray Fellow at the Woodstock Theological Center in Washington, D.C., and Franklin W. Knight was a Fellow at the Center for Advanced Study in the Behavioral Sciences at Stanford, California. We deeply appreciate the magnificent support of these institutions. Franklin Knight was directly supported during the calendar year 1977, and the academic year 1977/78 by The Johns Hopkins University, the National Endowment for the Humanities (grant number F 77/78 in 1977, and grant number FC 26278-76-1030 in 1978), and the Andrew W. Mellon Foundation. Dorothy Brothers of the Center for Advanced Study typed the final draft with welcome speed and efficiency. Houston Baker, Morton Bogdonoff, Jean Carew, Thomas Hunter, Ingeborg Bauer Knight, Manuel Moreno Fraginals, and Brian Smith influenced us in ways which were not always obvious to them but which substantially contributed to whatever fine qualities are found in our work. We assume, however, total responsibility for all shortcomings.

M. E. C.
F. W. K.

Africa and the Caribbean

1

THE AFRICAN MIGRATION
AND THE ORIGINS
OF AN AFRO-AMERICAN
SOCIETY AND CULTURE

Franklin W. Knight and
Margaret E. Crahan

The centuries-old link between Africa and the New World began in the Caribbean as an integral part of the expansion of Europe. In many ways the Caribbean provides the most appropriate scene for examining the legacies of that link. Nowhere else in the Americas are those legacies stronger and more pervasive. Nowhere else have the societies been more consistently fluid and the cultures more unfailingly dynamic than in this region that has been described as "the proscenium of American history."[1] In 1492 the Caribbean became the umbilical cord that nurtured the first attempts to transport and transform European societies across the Atlantic Ocean. It also provided the great paradox of the American experience as both a microcosm of things past as well as a harbinger of things to come. Throughout the not-too-distant past of the bold sailing ships, the Caribbean was the American Mediterranean and main gateway. Before the technological revolutions of the nineteenth century destroyed the "tyranny of distance"[2] and metaphorically brought both sides of the Atlantic World closer together, the Carribbean welcomed all, experienced all, affected all, and bid adieu to all those who chose to leave. Settlers, sojourners, exploiters, servants, and slaves traversed its seas, cleared its forests, forged new communities, and interrelated freely in a great variety of ways. More than any place else in the hemisphere, the Caribbean

1

was the great melting pot, the enchanting magnet for footloose noblemen as well as starving peasants, the amazing catalyst that unpredictably changed both the dreamers and their dreams.

For nearly four hundred years, the most visible aspect of the connection between Africa and the New World was the existence of a massive migration conducted as a commerce in human beings. Unfortunately, for far too long the ramifications of transatlantic slave trade remained the end of intellectual curiosity about Africa. The result has been an abysmally superficial understanding of the impact of Africa on the evolution of American societies. The slave trade existed legally between 1518 and at least 1860, and is documented in a voluminous, often technically excellent, and readily available literature. If there is still no general agreement on the number of Africans sold in the Americas, there is less dispute over the scope of the trade today than there was just a few years ago.[3] The literature on the slave trade is not equaled quantitatively or qualitatively by studies on the African societies from which the Africans were induced, forced, dragged, or suborned into slavery, or the transatlantic societies into which they were eventually incorporated and to which they made substantial contributions. The main cause of this discrepancy is not hard to find. The slave trade represented an enormous international commerce involving individual entrepreneurs as well as the assets and resources of some of the most powerful nation-states in Europe and the world. Its conduct, maintenance, and eventual dismantling intimately involved the main institutions of European and colonial politics.

To the operators of the slave trade, the African as merchandise was far more important than the African as person. Until the nineteenth century, European imperialists termed Africa "the Dark Continent," and the unfavorable connotations of that adjective were indelibly stamped on the public mind. The description of Africa as "dark" represented a deliberate attempt to evoke a negative, threatening picture of an area of people devoid of knowledge, understanding, and culture, backward, primitive, unrefined, ignorant, and possessing evil traits and desires. This idiomatic denigration of Africa—the pun derives from the unavoidable politics of language—responded to the political, social, and economic interests of pre-twentieth-century Europe. The political and economic power of Europe and its control of the most efficient technical devices of transportation and communication assured wide dissemination of their ethnocentric views among those societies that they influenced.

The result of this European cultural hegemony meant that popular concepts of race, culture, geography, and society reflected more the standardized images created and promulgated by the small body of elite nationalists than the realities of the everyday lives of the masses, even among predominantly Afro-American communities. Until recently academic interest in African culture was considered unworthy of the best scholars. Not surprisingly, therefore, the masses were strongly encouraged to regard manifest "Africanisms" in less than kindly light, and the personal experience of Judith Bettelheim described in Chapter 5 indicates that the recent arrival of nationalism has not entirely reversed the teachings of three hundred years of English colonialism among the Jamaican masses. Moreover, the profusion of studies dealing with Africa and the Afro-American society has progressively widened the available data base without seriously refining and overhauling the popular images of Africa.

The basis for the bifurcation of an academic tradition and a popular one has both a historical and a psychological dimension. Both are related, although the precise nature of the relationship is extremely difficult to ascertain and articulate.

No one has dealt with the problem better, nor expressed it more cogently, than Philip D. Curtin. The first paragraph of his preface to *The Atlantic Slave Trade* politely understates yet adequately encapsulates the position of the professional historian:

> The Western historical tradition until recent decades was thoroughly ethnocentric and ill-adapted to the investigation of other societies—still less to considering historical processes that involved two or more societies. The slave trade was a commercial system to recruit forced workers in one society and transport them to another with a vastly different culture. Both Africans and Europeans participated in the trade, and both societies were deeply influenced by it; but Western involvement had certain peculiarities that have left their mark on later historiography. The European metropolis imported very few slaves for its own use. . . . The traditional national histories of European states therefore tend to view the slave trade as something peripheral to their own social and political development. This same parochial tradition of ethnocentric national history was transplanted to the Americas. There too, historians tended not to see the slave trade as a whole, but to concentrate on the one segment that brought workers to their particular region. Even within their national sector, historians have too often regarded the Afro-American community created by the trade as an alien body on the periphery of national life.[4]

The invidious selectivity to which Curtin refers here, and develops throughout his preface and his book, pertains not only to the transfer of European historical practices and methodologies. Selectivity is an essential part of all cultural transfer. The remarkable observation is why in an otherwise creative environment an ordinarily innovative American people could consistently display such marked lack of intellectual curiosity about a topic so germane to their own society. This is the problem that defies easy explanation and that probably will never be resolved until we understand much better than we currently do the operational processes of the human brain. In dealing with the reaction to the presence of Afro-Americans, however, we are dealing with two things concurrently: the general structure of politics, economics, and culture, which boldly outline the required and expected formal behavioral patterns; and the individual attitudes controlled by one's own psychological and neurological processes as provocatively outlined in Jacques Monod's stimulating work, *Chance and Necessity*.[5] The principal enigma, in essence, is why we ask certain questions, or alternatively, what governs our intellectual curiosity.

Apart from the biological and physiological stimuli that predispose human curiosity, we may find some simple, practical explanation, which, for convenience, we may call the cultural environment in which we operate. This environment substantially fashions our *perception* in the way Edward Brathwaite uses the term in his commentary in *Comparative Perspectives on Slavery in New World Plantation Societies*.[6]

The proper starting point, then, for any examination of the cultural environment—as indeed, for any study dealing with the links between Africa and the Caribbean—must be with the societies constructed as a result of the transatlantic slave trade. And in this it is imperative to deal not just with slavery as an abstract inhumane institution, but with people and the entire social complex of which slavery was a part. African slaves who came to the Americas were migrants, albeit migrating under peculiar circumstances. We will therefore deal with three aspects of the African connection with the Americas in general and the Caribbean in particular: the community of migrants; the Afro-American society; and the construction, reconstruction, or creation of an Afro-American culture. Who were the Africans shipped to the New World? Where did they come from? What situations did they encounter in the Americas? How many were there in each individual locality? When did they come? What happened to them? Today these seem like simple questions, but until about ten years ago the answers were not easily obtained.

Philip D. Curtin's *The Atlantic Slave Trade*, to which we referred earlier, greatly reduced the wild excesses of what he so graphically termed "the Numbers Game" by establishing not only a basis for the overall volume, but suggesting a *modus operandi* for calculating the proportion of those Africans transported during periods for which records were quite deficient. Curtin's estimate for the total number of Africans landed in the New World is a little less then ten million for the full duration of the trade—with a margin of error ranging between plus or minus twenty percent. As long as the exact figure can never be ascertained, the quest for mathematical accuracy as an end in itself becomes a rather unrewarding pursuit. Accepting a range between eight million—(on the low side) and twelve million (on the high side) allows for a profile that does not vary sufficiently to affect some useful observations that can be made about the transatlantic migration.

The first observation is that the Atlantic slave trade represented the largest known transfer of people in history prior to the nineteenth century. The logistic of the transfer had enormous ancillary technical and economic bene-fits for the European participants. Not only did Europeans provide the ships and the managerial personnel for the ocean segment of the voyages, but they generated most of the trade commodities and received by far the greatest proportion of the profit directly and indirectly flowing from slave-trading activities. It might be a gross exaggeration to declare that slavery caused or created the industrial revolution—and surely recent works of Roger Anstey and William A. Green argue strongly to the contrary.[7] It is reasonable, how-ever, to argue that the economics of slavery and the slave trade provided a powerful lubricant and indispensable catalyst for the industrial revolution in Europe.

The impact on Africa of this massive drain of people is hard to calculate. But with the publication of the outstanding edition by Suzanne Miers and Igor Kopytoff, *Slavery in Africa, Historical and Anthropological Perspec-tives*,[8] we are much less ignorant than we used to be. Certainly the removal of a significant proportion of the potentially most valuable age-group must have had a tremendous impact on those localized sectors of Africa where the drain was most pronounced. But as Miers and Kopytoff point out, the recruitment varied considerably. "The acquisition of people [in Africa for enslavement] then, was a process ranging from voluntary or peaceful transactions between neighboring groups to bilateral compulsory transfers, and, with increasing degrees of coercion and organization, to the large-scale entrepreneurship of raiding and war."[9] Apart from the sociopolitical implications for African statebuilding and economic development, the nature of slave acquisition, sale, and transfer created havoc with the normal process of cultural transmission and group identification observed among other migrant groups to the New World. Notwithstanding, it would require considerably more data than is currently available to make confident correlations between the raw volume of slave exports and the local African sociopolitical impact. Nor would socio-political impact be necessarily tantamount to cultural impact. It is possible for death, disease, famine, war, and dispersal to ravage a society demographically without inflicting permanent damage to either culture, social institutions, or political forms. The recent history of Ireland, France, Germany, India, or the history of the Jewish diaspora all tend to support this assertion. Across the Atlantic Ocean, the situation was equally complex.

Afro-Americanization took place in the Americas under the strong influences of three internally variegated cultural sources: Europe, Africa, and the Americas. In all three areas both the societies and the cultures were constantly undergoing change. Although Africans accompanied the early Iberian explorers to the New World, the former were quite probably born in Iberia, and culturally indistinct from their masters. Until about 1516, then, the earliest stages of Spanish domination and colonization in the Antilles brought together the conflict of only two cultures. But with the royal sanction of direct, controlled slave trading with the varied culture areas of the African coast the new arrivals began to represent elements of new cultures that sharply contrasted both with the Iberians as well as the indigenous Americans. Gradually the slave trade expanded, and the Afro-Iberians became inundated in the African stream. Within the emerging communities of the American frontier, African, European, and local American cultures merged, reacted, adapted, and eventually produced a new form of creole American culture. Afro-American culture remained as a variation of this process. The emergence of this new culture forms the basic premise to which Sidney Mintz and Richard Price address themselves in their extremely insightful pamphlet, *An Anthropological Approach to the Afro-American Past: A Caribbean Perspective.*[10]

The fact that Europe and Africa played such important roles in the development of an Afro-American culture ought not to obscure the reality that the new immigrants from the eastern side of the Atlantic did not encounter a cultural (or social) *tabula rasa* in the Caribbean or elsewhere across the Americas. The indigenous Americans whom Christopher Columbus mistakenly called Indians also made their social and cultural contributions to the novel emergent American society and culture. Harry Hoetink's discussion in chapter 2 contributes to our understanding of these intrinsic indigenous ingredients by breaking down the three cultural matrices of the Afro-American legacy into forms of anthroculture, socioculture, and ethnic group boundary.

As in the case of the African migration to the Americas, the impact of the Indian contribution depends on the size of the base population in 1492. Here again the "numbers game" debate familiar to scholars working on the African slave trade to the Americas also afflicts the demographic studies of the New World at the time of the first European and African incursions. Our purpose in reintroducing the question of the original population lies less in extending the controversy than in trying to assess realistically the nature of the cultural impact that the host socieities might have had on the later development of the African Creole Society.

Scholarly estimates on the size of the Antillean populations range from tens of thousands to more than eight million. The sharp divergence of views is most patent in the discussions concerning the aboriginal population of the island of Hispaniola, generally agreed to have been the most densely inhabited of all the Caribbean islands in 1492. Charles Verlinden proposes a figure of fewer than 60,000 Indians.[11] Angel Rosenblat strongly argues for a total of no more than 100,000.[12] Julian Steward estimates some 225,000 persons in the *Handbook of South American Indians* as representative of the population of the Antilles as a whole.[13] These three figures appear to be on the conservative side. By contrast, Carl Sauer adamantly insists on his estimate of about three million for Hispaniola, while Sherburne F. Cook and Woodrow Borah have calculated a figure of between seven and eight million—and have thereby sparked even greater controversy than their earlier calculation of twenty-five million for the Central Valley of Mexico.[14] Franklin W. Knight's contribution to the debate is a rather nonscientifically derived estimate of approximately three-quarters of a million persons for all the Antilles, with the greatest proportion on Hispaniola, about 50,000 on Cuba, 45,000 on Puerto Rico, and about 20,000 on Jamaica.[15] The basis for this figure stems from the absence of descriptions among the earliest chroniclers of any evidence of massive destruction of the forest covers, or descriptions of large cities (except for Hispaniola), or later of significant gatherings of the bones of the dead.

Agreement on the decline of the indigenous population after the Spanish occupation of the Antilles is more general. The best summaries of the literature may be found in Carl Sauer's *Early Spanish Main* and William M. Denevan's *Native Population of the Americas in 1492*.[16] The precipitous scale of this decline is quite striking. As early as 1510, the Dominican priests had already observed and remarked on the dramatic decline of the population of Hispaniola. The conversion of Bartolomé de las Casas and his campaign to save the Indians from destruction added impetus to their laments and erratic wildness to the estimates not only of the local population but the nature of the decline.[17] By the middle of the sixteenth century the decline was an obvious, indisputable fact commonly accepted even by the Spanish metropolitan government.

The first reliable census of the Spanish Antilles proper was not until 1570. At that time the total inhabitants of the Spanish sphere was given as 85,650 individuals, settled in twenty-four legally recognized towns. This figure was not equivalent to the population of the Caribbean by any measure. A large number of Indians—of whom the fierce Caribs of the Lesser Antilles were the most notorious—were excluded from the Spanish count. Nevertheless, as equally important as the location of the Spanish sphere among the Greater Antilles was the composition of these Spanish towns. For this Spanish-controlled group comprised only 8,500 Spanish (9 percent), 22,150 Indians (26 percent), and a variegated melange of Africans, mestizos, and mulattoes amounting to about 56,000 (65 percent)—and which would probably fit under the current United States Census Bureau's euphemistic classification as "other."

This population profile is interesting and important from the perspective of culture and cultural transmission. Admittedly we know very little about the basis of the designations used by the Spanish in composing their census of 1570. But it is not unreasonable to suggest that the main criteria were cultural rather than biological, and that the Spanish incorporated many Indians into the "other" category for the Antilles simply on the basis of their dress or phenotype, as Aguirre Beltran established for Mexico during the same period.[18] If this hypothesis is correct, the extent of the demise of the local Indians within the context of Spanish colonial society might be less dramatic than the figures of the separate groups indicate. In any case, it suggests the possibility that the Indians could have influenced tremendously the cultural complex into which they were being inexorably submerged.

In the unfamiliar environment of the Americas, both Europeans and Africans must have borrowed freely in the uneven exchange necessary for the survival of the fledgling colonies. We have evidence of the acceptance by the recently arrived colonists of some aspects of the material culture of the Indians—their food crops, hammocks, utensils, and architectural styles.[19] Such adoption gradually became part of the local culture, and in some cases, even gained acceptance in the metropolis. Other aspects of the nonmaterial culture were also accepted, although the evidence so far is scanty—as it was bound to be for the less cultivated classes, especially the slaves. In the Caribbean, the emergent Afro-American society fashioned its patterns of social conduct, behavior, and thought not only from its African and European antecedents, but from the local, Indian host culture as well.

By the end of the sixteenth century, Africans and Europeans had already forged new societies and new cultures along the new American frontier. Another century brought vast changes. The frontier of predominantly European cultures was being transmuted as the agricultural revolutions on the tropical lowlands, the African immigration, and the rapid increase on the mestizo or mixed population, did in fact, create a new American type.

It is imperative to repeat at this point the cautious observation that, despite what Melville Herskovits and others have implied, cultural legacies from Africa cannot be traced in a linear fashion forward or backward.[20] Mintz and Price deal with this problem in great detail, concluding that "if Afro-American cultures do in fact share such an integral dynamism, and if, as we shall argue, their social systems have been highly responsive to changing social conditions, one must maintain a skeptical attitude toward claims that many contemporary social or cultural forms represent direct continuities from the African homelands."[21] Harry Hoetink expresses the same idea with impressive economy and conviction when he writes in chapter 2, "the vehicular forms [of cultural elements] as they emerged in the Caribbean area are *sui generis* both in their variety and per variety." In short, the Afro-Caribbean cultures derived from a variety of cultural models, and reflected a broad spectrum of local prevailing circumstances in their new habitat. The same point is made by Maureen Warner Lewis in her discussion of the literary and linguistic influences of the Caribbean in chapter 6. Regardless of the academic field, the nature of the connections and the process of transmission present main problems. Nevertheless, as Barry Higman points out in chapter 3, "few scholars have argued for a genuine continuity of African forms among the black population." The sum of these literary admonitions is that no basis exists for concluding from the suggestive data that practices and customs found commonly on both sides of the Atlantic Ocean are directly connected by a sort of simple linear borrowing one way or the other. The facile assumption of cultural parallels between the Caribbean and the non-Caribbean area undermines the intrinsic dynamism and creativity of the respective societies and leads to some of the problems that Judith Bettelheim encountered in her research in the Caribbean, especially pertaining to the *fanal* festival tradition (see chapter 5).

To acknowledge the difficulty of analyzing the forms of cultural transmission and the nature of cultural evolution by no means denies the importance of an African tradition (or traditions) within an Afro-American culture area. In fact, scholars such as Herbert Gutman and Miguel Barnet are beginning to indicate a far greater and more complex African impact in that predominantly tropical area from the Chesapeake Bay in the north, through the Caribbean to the mid-Atlantic coast of Brazil, within the region that nineteenth-century travelers conventionally called Afro-America.

Throughout the Caribbean, no direct correlation exists between the absolute size of the African and Afro-American populaton and the strength, cohesiveness, and pervasiveness of variants of a discernible Afro-American culture. This observation further weakens the probability of a linear transmission of African cultures to the New World and raises a number of questions about the nature and extent of African influences and the relationship between society and culture. Any attempt to come to terms with this relationship inevitably confronts three dominant factors in the evolution of Afro-American society: the volume of Africans imported; the pace of imports or time span during which the imports were made, or the immigration took place; and the socioeconomic structure of the recipient American society and culture. These factors are, of course, all interrelated.

Among the many attractive features of Philip Curtin's work, *The Atlantic Slave Trade*, is the facility that it affords for an assessment of a realistic flow of the volume of Africans entering the New World. Apart from the early sixteenth century, as we implied before (and the period during and after the nineteenth century, when a number of European states were dismantling their segment of the South Atlantic System), the flow of Africans to the New World was one of involuntary immigrants, of commercial slaves. This volume responded to the economic and demographic vicissitudes of the transatlantic slave trade. The Caribbean islands comprised the largest single recipient area for these Africans, accepting about 43 percent of all Africans sold in the Western Hemisphere.[22] Brazil, the second most popular destination, accounted for about 38 percent. The mainland Spanish-American colonies bought about 6 percent; while the English North American zone (later, the United States of America and Canada) handled about 4.5 percent of the total trade. These figures probably contain some margin of error, but the relative proportional participation over the entire history of the trade as outlined by Curtin has remained substantially unchallenged. The Caribbean and Brazil, especially the northeast of Brazil, provided the homes—and the graves—for approximately 80 percent of all the Africans shipped to the New World.

The conditions of transit for these Africans were not conducive to the coordinated transfer of a total African culture, even had such an integral culture existed. The African transatlantic migration derived from the necessities of cheap labor and profitable commerce and was not designed for the aid, comfort, and community of the migrants. As such, the stream of immigrants was more age- and sex-specific—while being more culturally heterogeneous—than any other group migrating to the New World. Nevertheless, given the diffuse nature of origin and the variety of local situations into which the African was eventually placed on arrival in the Americas, it was improbable, but not impossible, for specific groups to be reconstituted overseas. The point to be emphasized, however, is that reconstitution of any specific ethnic group overseas did not necessarily re-create the original conditions for the propagation of the basic African culture in all its authentic dimensions. For we are dealing not with free individuals in families, but with slaves in slavery. Volume and specific group dominance, therefore, were affected by the pace of introduction, and the socioeconomic situation into which African immigrants fitted on their arrival in the Americas.

As previously mentioned, the pace of introduction responded closely to market demands in the Western Atlantic, although war and commerce between the European nation-states resulted in serious disruptions. But if we take the gross figures, we can still get a graphic picture of the overall flow. Using the Curtin figures, we get approximately seventy-five thousand brought to all of Spanish America (including the Antilles), and an additional fifty thousand introduced to Brazil during the sixteenth century. Some of these Africans came via Iberian ports, and the average flow was at the relatively low rate of about twelve hundred Africans per year. Such a low general demand regionally coincided with pockets of high demand such as those Caribbean islands where the indigenous population had been decimated. Hispaniola was the best example of this occurrence in the sixteenth century. But the low supply/demand reflected other characteristics of the trade which would greatly diminish or disappear later. One of these early characteristics was that purchasers were more fastidious about the origin of their merchandise, resulting in a process of selection which might have resulted in relatively dense concentrations of certain African ethnic groups. French Guiana, as illustrated by the Remire Sugar Estate records of 1690, seems to substantiate this point.[23] Low incoming rates probably coincided with ethnic and culturally cohesive cohorts and allowed the establishment of certain societal norms to which later arrivals, regardless of their custom, would have to conform. Changes in the rate and volume could affect, modify, or change the cultural patterns as in the cases of Cuba and Jamaica, or merely create a melange as in the case of Trinidad.

What precisely constituted an ethnic group, however, remains a major historiographical problem, although probably more common among anthropologists than historians. Some of the ethnic denominations in the literature are clearly arbitrary. Some merely reflect our contemporary confusion and frustration at trying to understand the ways of the past. Manuel Moreno Fraginals articulates this observation with commendable precision when he writes:

> Our basic assumption is that the slave trade was the business that involved the greatest amount of capital investment in the world, during the eighteenth and nineteenth centuries. And a business of this size would never have kept up a classificatory scheme had it not been meaningful (in overall general terms in keeping with reality) in designating in a *very precise* way the merchandise that was being traded. The fact that the term used by the traders in the past does not today have the same meaning is another problem and does not invalidate the fact that it was initially meaningful. To give just one example, we know from the many documents that the family name *Congo* referred to a concrete ethnic grouping (with a con-

crete language, culture and mode of conduct), even though today that same term refers to a vast geographical region and whole complex of people and cultures.[24]

Specific ethnic identification did not necessarily indicate the retention of the formerly associated ethnic culture. Both the fluidity of the American frontier and the relatively small size of the slave holding (or even the pro-portional disparity between Africans and non-Africans) served to undermine the cohesive articulation and prolonged retention of any specific African eth-nic culture. Representative ethnic cultures survived, but without necessarily reflecting closely the basic original mix of the African locality or region.

Sexual composition and timing of entry were important considerations for both the society and the culture. As the plantation society expanded throughout the Caribbean, the volume of the Africans entering the region increased dramatically. The incoming stream increased from 1.4 million in the seventeenth century, to nearly six million in the eighteenth century, and declined to about two million during the nineteenth century. The average annual importation increased from two thousand in 1600, to thirteen thou-sand in 1700, and an astonishing fifty-five thousand in 1810. From that high point, with the increased British naval and diplomatic activity to end the slave trade, the volume diminished gradually until its virtual disappearance by 1870. The entire South Atlantic System collapsed during the nineteenth century from a variety of internal and external causes.

The development of an Afro-American culture within the context of an Afro-American society was either facilitated or inhibited by the number and proportion of the female sector of the incoming group. Women, after all, do form the integral link in the process of socialization and cultural trans-mission. In this respect, therefore, both the sexual composition of the ar-rivals as well as the sexual differences of the basic host group would have an undetermined effect on the evolution of the society and the culture. We can discuss this sexual dimension in two ways: first, from the perspective of the trade; and second, from the perspective of the American-born, or Creole, population.

Before the late eighteenth century the incoming African slave popula-tion consisted predominantly of male adults. The initial high demand, coupled with the general belief that males were more effective at clearing the forests and establishing the plantations resulted in about 80 percent of all early arrivals being male Africans. Gradually, however, a combination of factors led to a marked increased in the number and proportion of women: the requirements of social control, the increase in the price of male slaves; the international attacks on the slave trade; and the discovery or rationalization that women were just as effective on the plantations as men. Moreno Fraginals has charted the sex distribution among the African slaves on selected Cuban estates between 1746 and 1868.[25] His sample demonstrates that between 1748 and 1790 males comprised 90.38 percent of the African labor force. This proportion fell to 85.03 percent between 1791 and 1822; 69.7 percent between 1823 and 1844; and 59.8 percent between 1845 and 1868. In the Cuban case, the pressures to abolish the slave trade proved to be one of the chief destabilizing factors in the trade, thereby accentuating the increase in the female proportion from less than 10 percent in the initial period, to more than 40 percent by 1868. Higman's study for nineteenth-century Jamaica confirms the general sex profile of Moreno Fraginals for Cuba. Higman estimates that during the last period of the trade to Jamaica, "the proportion of males imported [was] unlikely to have exceeded 60 percent of the total."[26] For Cuba, Moreno Fraginals found that "during the decade of the 1820's, four out of every ten immigrants were women; during the decade of the 1830's, the figure rose to five out of every ten . . . [and] around 1850 . . . out of every fifteen immigrants, seven were women."[27]

In every slave society, the stabilization of the plantation frontier coincided with changes in the demographic structure of the African and Afro-American population. These changes were most pronounced in the sex balance, age profile, and Creole proportion of the cohorts, declines in the mortality and morbidity rates, and a general population pyramid approximating that of any normal organic population group. These changes can be illustrated by the figures for Cuba (or for anywhere else) where the creole sector of the slave labor force increased from 11.53 percent in the later eighteenth century to 47.02 percent by 1868. In the English and French Antilles, as well as the United States of America, Creoles formed the dominant group of all large slave holdings during the nineteenth century.

Across the Americas the volume of slave imports tended to diminish with the growth of a Creole Afro-American population. The most extreme case of this is found in the United States of America. There the approximately 427,000 slaves imported (largely before 1790) increased to approximately 4.5 million Afro-Americans by 1864. But these Afro-Americas were creolized in a society in which they formed a minority of the population. The black population in the United States might have comprised about 40 percent of all the black population in the hemisphere, but it constituted a paltry 7 percent of the total population in the United States. The increases in the proportion of creoles produced a series of collateral changes in the structure of the Afro-American society. The number of children increased, suggesting a higher natality rate; social mores differed from the predominantly African-born society; family structure and relationships as well as occupational roles changed, as Higman suggests in his study of the case of Trinidad.[28] Naturally, creolization within the context of a minority group would have some important effects on the development of a socioculture, effects which might not be duplicated within the majority context of the greater number of Caribbean situations.[29]

Outside the United States of America a high mortality rate during the years of slavery was typical. The Caribbean islands altogether imported nearly five million slaves during the period from 1518 to 1870, yet the combined population in 1880 slightly exceeded two million. The individual cases illustrate the decline even more graphically. The English colony of Jamaica imported a net total of more than six hundred thousand Africans during the eighteenth century. In 1834 the African and Afro-American population was less than 350,000. Between 1715 and 1780 the planters of the French colony of Saint-Domingue bought more than 800,000 Africans. Yet, in 1790, on the eve of the great rebellion, the total Afro-American population was only 500,000. In the Spanish colony of Cuba, some 600,000 Africans were brought in to create their large scale sugar and coffee plantations between 1810 and 1860, but the Afro-American sector numbered a scant 528,798—and that thanks mainly to the fertility of the substantial free Afro-American sector on the island.

Large, concentrated immigration of Africans indicated a more heterogenous source in Africa than small, dispersed importations. Coupled with the abnormally high mortality rates, the surviving population was forced to be even more culturally eclectic than might be expected. An "African culture," therefore, could not survive as a distinguishable, cohesive entity, although elements of such culture would of necessity have to survive, given the situation in which the arrivals found themselves.

This situation was the variegated socioeconomic structure of the Americas, and for the vast majority of Africans, this meant plantation America. The two dominant structural complexes along this socioeconomic continuum have been described with only slight distortion as settler societies and exploitation societies.[30] The labels reflect the aspirations and achievements of the managerial European component, but it was within this essentially European matrix that the Africans would retain, adapt, create, and forge their complementary Afro-American culture.

Exploitation colonies afforded Africans more control of their daily lives and interpersonal relationships, although, paradoxically, their servitude was often more coerced and constrained than in settler societies. The white proportion of the population in these former societies was often too small to supply an effective dominant cultural role model. Moreover, as Franklin

W. Knight has argued:

> Exploitation societies. . . lacked a common, unifying institutional basis. They were ad hoc societies—innovative only for self-preservation. Not only were such societies divided, they tended to be divisive, with mutually reinforcing cleavages within the castes. However long the [white] elite remained physically *in situ*, they were psychologically transients, with a myopic confusion of social order and productive efficiency. The most enduring and sometimes the most interesting features of the society were created by the lower classes, who were often told what they could not do but rarely what they ought to do.
>
> Nevertheless, the cultural weaknesses and deficiencies of the plantation elite provided an almost unique opportunity for the coerced African element to help fashion a society.[31]

The individual history and specific prevailing circumstances precluded a direct correlation between what we can today discern as viable "African retentions" on the one hand, and the proportion of Europeans in the population on the other. Notwithstanding it is interesting to review the demographic profile of these colonies during the nineteenth century. A random sample will suffice.[32] In English Grenada, the 771 whites formed 2.5 percent of the colony's total population of 31,362, and 39 percent of those free in 1811. In Trinidad, acquired by the English in 1797, the whites totaled 4,353 in 1811, forming 13.3 percent of the island population of 32,664 and 36.7 percent of the free. In Dutch Surinam the whites numbered 2,500 in 1830, accounting for 4.4 percent of the colony, and 33.2 percent of the free. In French Martinique in 1789, the 10,636 white inhabitants comprised 11 percent of the colonial population of 96,158, and 66.7 percent of the free. Other cases, however, did not produce such extreme ratios. The 4,755 whites on Bermuda formed 48 percent of the total of 9,900 in 1812, and 91.3 percent of the free. In Cuba the 311,051 whites in 1827 amounted to 44.1 percent of the total of 704,487, and 74.5 percent of the free. In Puerto Rico, the 300,406 whites in 1860 comprised 51.5 percent of the island total of 583,181 and 55.5 percent of the free population. Neither Bermuda nor Puerto Rico represented classical cases of the exploitation slave society, however, and Cuba falls into what Hoetink calls his "two-phase" recipient colonies. Overall, the white sector varied from less than 3 percent in Berbice and Grenada to the 51.5 percent in Puerto Rico, with the average proportion of whites falling in the vicinity of 10 percent.

What is clear from the above figures is that the proportion of whites was small not only in proportion to the total regional population, but also in absolute terms, except in those French and Spanish colonies where vestiges of the settler society persevered. Jamaica, the largest English island colony had only about 15,000 whites in a total population of 340,000 in 1800.[33] Demerara, a frontier sugar colony, had slightly more than 2,000 white persons in a population of more than 57,000. The social class and sexual composition of this white sector was often as varied as among the slave groups. Moreover, the fluctuating fortunes of European imperialism produced what to recent African arrivals must have seemed a patent babel of languages and customs, in which a lingua franca became essential. The experience in Trinidad illustrates this point. The 4,353 whites in Trinidad in 1811 represented ten separate national identities: Spanish (559 or 12.8 percent), French (681 or 15.6 percent), American Indians (1,736 or 39.8 percent), English (1,280 or 29.4 percent), Americans from the United States (20), Germans (25), Portuguese (4), Italians (18), Corsicans (20), and Maltese (10). Such a situation of commingled cultures and nationalities has led some scholars, for example the sociologist Orlando Patterson, to the rash conclusion that these plantation-exploitation structures did not comprise societies.[34] Integral societies as in Europe they most certainly were not. But they were undeniably exploitation societies and Afro-American societies.

Yet, if the whites were few, their political and economic power was great. Afro-Caribbean societies would never escape the indelible impressions of European imperialism and colonialism. During the long period of the social disintegration, reconstruction, and nation building that took place throughout the Caribbean in the nineteenth and twentieth centuries, the legacies of Africa became distorted, diluted, and subordinated. The communication between both sides of the topical Atlantic dwindled and virtually disappeared. What was worse, the African legacy became related to an inferior status even among the predominantly Afro-Caribbean societies. A conflict developed between the Eurocentric goals and attitudes of the proponents of high culture and the mass-based, Afro-American low culture. In one form or the other, this conflict—especially evident in language and literature—has plagued Caribbean societies to the present day. Colonialism might have succeeded in driving underground the strong appeal of Africa throughout the Caribbean. It could not, and did not, destroy the bonds between the two regions. As ideal, refuge, and solace, an image of Africa remained alive and well among the descendants of that continent in the New World. It remained vital because the African origins could not be entirely expunged from those fundamental areas of society and culture which form the backbone of every community and that are expresssed in its religion, its language, and its literature. We have tried to touch on these aspects in this collection.

The examples discussed by Monica Schuler, Maureen Warner Lewis, and Lorna Williams may at first appear to be too localized in their particular case studies of Jamaica Myalism, Anglo-Caribbean linguistic structure and literary application, and the psychological and political usage of Africa in the poetry of Nicolás Guillén.[35] But the problems discussed by these authors are not unique. Rather, they are representative of certain Caribbean problems which transcend linguistic and national boundaries.[36] Guillén has his French-speaking counterpart in Frantz Fanon and his English-speaking counterpart in Vic Reid. Africa is an inescapable fact of Caribbean life and society. Moreover, political independence within the region and the general political environment in the contemporary world have gone far to restore the respectability of Africa and the legitimacy of the intellectual pursuit of African themes. Fidel Castro's public declaration in the 1970s that Cuba was an Afro-Latin American state served to alleviate the weighty loneliness with which Haitians have had to struggle for nearly two centuries. Political rhetoric, however, does not miraculously change the reality. Political sympathy and genealogy do not suffice to remove the misunderstandings of the past and present—as the imaginal confusion manifest in such varied sources as the ideology of Marcus Garvey, the Rastafarians and the poetry of Nicolás Guillén suggest. The common hope behind the authors of these original essays is to make a modest contribution to that understanding, and to provide a preliminary base and an incentive for further research and writing. More we cannot ask. Less we dare not attempt. The task of reconciling history and reality, intellectual images and popular conceptions never ends.

NOTES

1. See Dolores M. Martin, "Close Encounters of the Third World," *The Washington Post Book World*, 22 January 1978, p. 1.

2. The phrase is taken from the title of that marvelous book by Geoffrey Blainey, *The Tyranny of Distance: How Distance Shaped Australia's History* (London, 1975).

3. The best scholarly treatment of the entire slave trade remains that of Philip D. Curtin, *The Atlantic Slave Trade: A Census* (Madison, Wis., 1969). For revisions of some aspects of the Curtin figures, see Stanley L. Engerman and Eugene D. Genovese, eds., *Race and Slavery in the Western Hemisphere: Quantitative Studies* (Princeton, 1975); Enriqueta Vila Vilar, *Hispanoamérica y el comercio de esclavos. Los asientos portugueses* (Seville, 1977); as well as idem, "Los asientos Portugueses y el contrabando de Negros," *Anuario de Estudios Américanos* 30 (1973): 557-609; and the essays included in Vera Rubin and Arthur Tuden, eds., *Comparative Perspectives on Slavery in New World Plantation Societies* (New York, 1977); David Eltis, "The Traffic in Slaves between the British West Indian Colonies, 1807-1833," *Economic History Review*, 25 (February

1972): 55-64; D. R. Murray, "Statistics of the Slave Trade to Cuba, 1790-1867," *Journal of Latin American Studies* (1971): 131-49.

4. Curtin, *Slave Trade*, p. xv.

5. Jacques Monod, *Chance and Necessity: An Essay on the Natural Philosophy of Modern Biology* (New York, 1971).

6. Rubin and Tuden, *Comparative Perspectives*, p. 43.

7. Roger Anstey, *The Atlantic Slave Trade and British Abolition, 1760-1810* (Atlantic Highlands, New Jersey, 1975); William A. Green, *British Slave Emancipation: The Sugar Colonies and the Great Experiment, 1830-1865* (Oxford, 1976). Both books implicitly refute Eric Williams's *Capitalism and Slavery* (Chapel Hill, 1944).

8. Suzanne Miers and Igor Kopytoff, *Slavery in Africa: Historical and Anthropological* (Madison, Wis., 1977).

9. Miers and Kopytoff, *Slavery in Africa*, p. 14.

10. Sidney Mintz and Richard Price, *An Anthropological Approach to the Afro-American Past: A Caribbean Perspective* (Philadelphia, 1976).

11. Charles Verlinden, "Le 'repartimiento' de Rodrigo de Albuquerque a Espagnola en 1514: Aux origines d'une importante institution économico-sociale de l'empire colonial espagnol," in *Mélanges offerts à G. Jacquemyns*, ed. Charles Verlinden (Brussels, 1968), pp. 633-46.

12. Angel Rosenblat, *La población de América en 1492: Viejos y Nuevos Cálculos* (Mexico City, 1967).

13. Julian Steward, *The Handbook of South American Indians*, 7 vols. (Washington, D.C., 1949), 5:655-68.

14. Carl Sauer, *The Early Spanish Main* (Berkeley, 1966); Sherburne Cook and Woodrow Borah, *Essays in Population History: Mexico and the Caribbean*, 2 vols. (Berkeley, 1971-74), and their *The Population of the Mixteca Alta* (Berkeley, 1968).

15. Franklin W. Knight, *The Caribbean: The Genesis of a Fragmented Nationalism* (New York, 1978), pp. 5-15.

16. William M. Denevan, *The Native Population of the Americas in 1492* (Madison, Wis., 1976).

17. See, Angel Rosenblat, "The Population of Hispaniola at the Time of Columbus," in Denevan, *Native Population*, pp. 43-66.

18. Aguirre Beltran, *La población negra de México* (Mexico City, 1946).

19. Knight, *Caribbean*, pp. 15-19; Rosenblat, "Population of Hispaniola," passim.

20. Melville J. Herskovits, *The Myth of the Negro Past* (Boston, 1958).

21. Mintz and Price, *An Anthropological Approach*, p. 27.

22. All figures and percentages pertaining to the trade are taken or calculated from Curtin, *Atlantic Slave Trade*. See also, Franklin W. Knight, *The African Dimension in Latin American Societies* (New York, 1974).

23. Curtin, *Slave Trade*, p. 189.

24. Manuel Moreno Fraginals, "Africa in Cuba: A Quantitative Analysis of the African Population in the Island of Cuba," in Rubin and Tuden, *Comparative Perspectives*, pp. 187-201. The emphasis is that of the author.

25. Ibid., p. 192.

26. Barry W. Higman, *Slave Population and Economy in Jamaica, 1807-1833* (Cambridge, 1976), p. 72.

27. Moreno Fraginals, "Africa in Cuba," p. 193.

28. See chapter 3.

29. Compare for example, Edward Brathwaite, *The Development of Creole Society in Jamaica, 1770-1820* (Oxford, 1971), and Herbert G. Gutman, *The Black Family in Slavery and Freedom 1750-1925* (New York, 1976).

001,

30. See Franklin W. Knight, "Patterns of Colonial Society and Culture: Latin America and the Caribbean, 1492-1804," in *South Atlantic Studies*, ed. Jack R. Censer, N. Steven Steinert, and Amy M. McCandles, vol. 2 (Charleston, 1978), pp. 3-23.

31. Knight, *Caribbean*, p. 65.

32. Ibid., p. 238.

33. Higman, *Slave Population*, p. 144.

34. Orlando Patterson, *The Sociology of Slavery: An Analysis of the Origins, Development and Structure of Negro Slave Society in Jamaica* (London, 1967).

35. See chapters 4, 6, and 7.

36. See, for example, Manuel Alvárez Nazario, *El elemento afro-negroide en el español de Puerto Rico: Contribución al estudio del negro en América* (San Juan, Puerto Rico, 1961; reprinted 1974), and *idem, El influjo indígena en el español de Puerto Rico* (San Juan, 1977); Juan Pérez de la Riva, *Para la historia de la gente sin historia* (Barcelona, 1976); and Migene González-Wippler, *Santería: African Magic in Latin America* (New York, 1975).

2

THE CULTURAL LINKS

Harry Hoetink

The exploration of the historical links between the Caribbean and Africa during the last four hundred years demands a greater skill in the art of synthesis than I can hope to muster, for this is a subject on which a great amount of ink has been used, especially during the past two decades. For convenience and brevity I have chosen to point out some variables in the formation of Afro-American societies from which I will subsequently make some comparative observations.

In general, Africans transported to the Caribbean primarily formed a servile labor force for an internally varied regional plantation system which, within the framework of an international division of labor, mainly specialized in the mass production of either agrarian luxury products—sugar, tobacco, cacao, coffee—or raw materials for the metropolitan textile industry such as cotton and indigo. The only exceptions were the relatively small numbers of *esclavos de companía y servicio* (public and private slaves) introduced into the larger Spanish inlands during the earliest years of the sixteenth century, and who had probably already assimilated the Spanish language, religion, and culture, and who participated in the conquest or assisted in the process of early colonization.[1] Another exception was the equally small number of similarly sociologically interesting immigration of "free" Africans to some Caribbean areas in the nineteenth century.[2] African socialization in the Caribbean, therefore, took place within the framework of a society and a culture dominated by the plantation system.

In the various Caribbean societies, this plantation system developed and reached its apogee at different historical periods.

Sugar was the main agricultural end-product, and in some islands the development of the sugar plantation was a virtually uninterrupted process, during which changes in plantation size, in capital intensity, in technology, and in basic master-slave relations succeeded each other in the course of perhaps two centuries while the plantation system maintained itself as the dominant mode of production. In other Caribbean societies, however, we may distinguish at least two phases of development, separated by a clear "interregnum" during which sugar was not "king" at all. The difference in economic continuity between these two groups of societies is reflected in different intensities of slave immigration. And it is reflected as well in a large spectre of phenomena which may be subsumed under the nomer of differential incorporation of that part of the population of African origin.

The African immigration to the Caribbean falls, then, into two distinct patterns; each corresponding to the type of its plantation development. The first pattern applies, more or less, to the Greater Antilles—Cuba, Hispaniola, Jamaica, and Puerto Rico—which had a "two-phase" plantation system, and a "two-wave" slave immigration. During the first fifty years after the Spanish conquest, Santo Domingo and Cuba in particular experienced a proportionally massive first wave of slave immigration.[3]   Initially, these slaves were used for a variety of extractive, agrarian, and construction activities, but gradually they began to provide forced labor for the incipient sugar plantation system which, with its simple technology,[4] expanded considerably during the first half of the sixteenth century, losing its momentum afterwards with the depletion of the Spanish population as a result of the massive exodus to the newly conquered areas of the Spanish American mainland. The slaves on these islands during that period were sufficiently numerous, and the decline of the colonizing population at the end of the period sufficiently great, to have a very considerable part of the local populations in the early censuses defined as either "black" or "mixed." In addition, this great influx of African slaves occurred at a time when the Amerindians were still relatively numerous, resulting in a varied relationship with the latter which ranged from domination through coalition to revolt and marronage. After about 1550, economic stagnation slowly overtook these islands, providing an opportunity for the rural population, European, African, or Afro-Indian, to occupy the available land and convert itself into a stratum of subsistence peasants. Slavery prevailed, of course, de jure, but it was maintained de facto primarily in the few locations where the small sugar mills, or *trapiches*, needed forced labor for their effective operation.

The second phase of sugar-cane agriculture and sugar processing was technologically more advanced and on a larger scale than the first, and the second

wave of slave importation was far larger in absolute numbers. This phase began with the capture of Jamaica by the English in 1655 and its conversion
into a plantation society very soon thereafter. The first phases of the development of sugar production on both Jamaica and western Hispaniola had been
very weak under the Spanish domination. But Jamaica under the English, and
Saint-Domingue (as the French preferred to call their colony after it was
ceded in 1697) experienced quite intense second phases. In the case of Saint-
Domingue, this lasted throughout the eighteenth century until its premature
and abrupt termination by the Haitian Revolution that stopped the slave importation, obliterated the internal French colonial power structure, severely
damaged agricultural production, and placed the new nation (after 1804) in a
sui generis situation both in terms of international relations and in terms of
its internal social and racial structure. In Cuba the second wave of slave importation began about the 1760s and lasted until the 1860s, with slavery
itself terminated in 1886. In Puerto Rico the second phase started in the early
nineteenth century but lasted briefly, in great part because the population
density there made specific forms of forced internal labor recruitment
possible, thereby lessening the importance of slavery as a basis for the supply
of plantation manpower. Slavery, nevertheless, prevailed in Puerto Rico until
1873.[5] In the eastern part of Hispaniola (today, the Dominican Republic) the
second phase of sugar-cane agriculture did not start until the 1870s, when
slavery was already abolished. The manpower needs of the new plantations
there were supplied internally as well as from neighboring Haiti, and the
nearby, mostly British, Caribbean islands. This later type of recruitment,
from which Cuba also profited until well into the twentieth century, was
feasible because when the mature sugar plantation system arrived in these
essentially Hispanic islands, it had already begun a decline in the English and
French Antilles.

Within the category of two-phase sugar colonies, then, it is possible to
form three subgroupings of societal situations defined by the impact of each
phase and by the length of the intervening stagnation period; societies such as
Jamaica and Haiti where the first phase was weak and where a powerful
second phase started early; societies such as the Dominican Republic and
Puerto Rico where the first phase was followed by a long period of stagnation, with the second phase starting only in the nineteenth century, with
few Africans introduced as slaves in Puerto Rico, and none at all in the case
of the Dominican Republic; and, intermediate societies such as Cuba, where
the first phase was important, the stagnation period of medium length, and
the sugar revolution characterized by intensive cultivation and massive slave
importation.

If one were to argue that a strong first phase had great significance for the subsequent social and cultural development of the territory, the example of Cuba would assume great importance in demonstrating such a thesis. Like Puerto Rico and the Dominican Republic—especially the latter—Cuba had a strong first phase; and with Jamaica, it shared an intensive second wave of African immigration (which ended more than half a century earlier in Jamaica than in Cuba),[6] as I shall discuss later.

The second pattern of African slave immigration conforms to the development of the Lesser Antilles, the Guyanas, Northeastern Brazil, and what today is called the South in the United States of America, where cotton rather than sugar was the main plantation crop. These areas experienced a one-phase plantation development, accompanied by a virtually continuous slave immigration as long as the transatlantic slave trade was permitted, or as long as its prohibition could be rewardingly circumvented.

These two patterns do not encompass the range of American or Caribbean situations in which Africans were found either as slaves or as free individuals. Some islands were mainly trading posts while other areas had a subsistence economy. Yet the plantation economy and the slave immigration it engendered was an essential trait of the area as a whole.

The one-phase plantation economies varied perceptibly with regard to the period in which they began their development, as well as the duration of their slave systems and their slave immigrations. African slave immigration began in northeastern Brazil during the sixteenth century. Therefore that region belongs with the Guianas and the Lesser Antilles (excluding Trinidad) with their early-seventeenth-century beginnings to the group of early starters. In sharp contrast with the other regions, however, where slave importation ended in the early nineteenth century, Brazil was, of all the societies under discussion, the last zone effectively to end the slave trade. At the other extreme, Trinidad probably passed through the shortest period of African slave immigration. As a sparsely populated Spanish colony, Trinidad turned to the plantation-style cultivation of the sugar cane at the end of the eighteenth century mainly under the initiative of French-Creole migrant planters. After 1797, the English gave fresh impetus to the expansion of the plantations. The end of the English transatlantic slave trade in 1808 cut off the African labor supply, but by the middle of the nineteenth century, the island had begun to substitute East Indians indentureds on the sugar estates. In the Southern United States the cotton plantation labor demand expanded at just about the time that Trinidad entered the sugar complex. But a large part of this mainland demand was supplied internally from other areas of British North America and the United States where the importations had occurred earlier. The African slave labor importation to the South lasted until the abrupt abolition of the slave system during the Civil War in 1863. (This abolition coincided with that of the Netherland Antilles, was later than Great Britain [1833], and France [1848], and was much later than Haiti [1804] and the Dominican Republic [1821]. But the abolition of slavery in the United States of America preceded that of Spain [Puerto Rico, 1873; Cuba, 1880], or Brazil [1888].)

In the British and French possessions, the dominant sugar plantation system succeeded a stage of small farming, peasant-like operations which depended less on Africans than on European indentureds and *engagés*. During the transition to the sugar cane monoculture, these indentureds initially worked together with and often alongside the imported African slaves, but they were gradually sieved out of the new system. In Brazil, on the other hand, the plantations provided for a contact situation similar to the one observed on the larger Spanish islands as a whole: black and Amerindian slaves initially coexisted, with the latter gradually disappearing from the slave system. Yet the contacts between the two population groups—outside the plantation and outside of slavery—were never entirely severed.

Nonwhite peasant activities emerged in symbiotic relationship with the plantation economy in these "one phase" plantation societies.[7] Their market system depended to some extent on the fluctuations in sugar prices, and hence on the plantations' need for land and labor. Overall the strength of peasant economies depended on the weakness of the plantation system's sociopolitical structure.

Where, after abolition, the sugar economy still seemed to be economically attractive, and labor scarcity persisted even after massive immigration of East Indian or other contract labor, as in British Guiana,[8] the efforts of former slaves to establish themselves as small farmers were strongly opposed by the dominant planter class, anxious to maintain its pool of cheap dependent labor. Where, as in Jamaica, the decline of sugar after abolition (and even before) seemed definite, a black peasant stratum of considerable size did emerge.

Isolated settlements of Maroons came into being much earlier wherever physical enviroment and scale lent themselves to the preservation of quasi-autonomous, self-protected communities of runaway slaves, in Brazil, Surinam, Jamaica, Cuba, Santo Domingo (to where in the eighteenth century many slaves from Saint Domingue fled).[9] On the smaller islands, a successful flight for a slave nearly always meant escape over sea to another colony.

Taking the one-phase plantation economies as a category, we may conclude that the variety among them precludes any internal classification along clear-cut lines. Due to their long and continuous experience with slavery and slave immigration and their virtually total dedication to sugar cultivation, the proportion of the population of African origin came to be larger than in those islands with a strong first phase and a medium-to-long stagnation period: the Greater Antilles, minus Jamaica and Haiti.

An exception is Trinidad, which underwent, as did British Guiana and Surinam, a massive immigration of Asian contract labor in the course of the nineteenth century.

In the above sketchy outline, the *physical* links between Africa and the Caribbean have been implied. The variety in strength and duration of these physical links for each society can be measured in part by analyzing the varying intensity of the slave trade and immigration as has been tried, explicitly and quantitatively, by several authors.[10]

What interests us here is the question of the extent to which these physical links, in close interplay with the varying demographic, ecological, and economic environments of Caribbean societies (some of which have already been alluded to) contributed to a kind of continuity at a cultural level. It is the old, but again crucial and unavoidable, question about the meaning of "Africanism" to which an essay such as this inevitably has to direct itself, and the questions about subjective and objective continuity after most physical links have been terminated. It would seem that the ongoing debate on Africanism and Africanness[11] would be served, if we were to develop distinct concepts of culture, each tied to specific social configurations, and if we might be able to indicate the processes by which configuration and culture evolve from one to another kind.

In the present-day sociological theory, in which the development and consequences of division of labor take a prominent place, the usual concept of culture is tied closely to and derived from the stratification produced by a given division of labor. In this sense, culture is linked to class. Thus, in this line of thought, working-class culture is conceived as a set of norms, expectations, internal social relations (family forms, relations between sexes and age groups), and external relations (attitudes and behavior vis-à-vis other classes), which all, in principle, evolve from class situations as such, even though specific demographic, economic, and ecological characteristics may lead to internal variations within the same class in any given society. Such a concept of culture, viewed as a function of social position, we might call here socioculture.[12]

On the other hand, traditional anthropology uses a concept of culture that—as the term "cultural heritage" implies—transcends momentary divisions of labor and hence social classes, and indicates—in a more durable sense than is the case with socioculture—all that is characteristic, i.e., both common to and distinctive of, a social system as a whole. In other words, this anthroculture emphasizes those systems of communication (language, religion), and regulating principles (of kinship, of succession) which have a boundary defining character vis-à-vis other social systems. It stresses the cultural properties that identify in a durable manner any social system—usually in its own political territory. Anthroculture thus defines one's identity as a member of a given society. Socioculture, by contrast, is defined by a social class's position within a given society. Seen in this manner, it is clear that within a social system, and its boundary defining anthroculture, several sociocultures may exist, each corresponding to one of the functional strata, produced by the system's division of labor. Within such a system and its territory, regional variations in anthroculture will also occur. But the boundary-marking functions of the system's anthroculture imply ideally and by definition, that such internal variations in *their* boundary marking effects will be subordinated to those of the system as a whole, in their members' perception.

It is possible that under certain conditions, e.g., a persistent stasis of the social system, the socioculture of a given stratum "solidifies" into an anthroculture. Thus, the socially (class) determined variations in language, religion, and other attributes of communication and presentation may, often through a long social isolation of a stratum, crystallize into anthrocultural characteristics. These, added to the isolated stratum's endogamy which makes descent one of its other boundary-marking attributes, will convert the original functional stratum (class) into an *ethnie*. But such a rare process of social and cultural hardening (which nevertheless did occur in some caste-like societies), only serves to illustrate that it is possible to construct a genetic connection between socioculture and anthroculture, and that a particular anthroculture may be limited to one functional stratum only.

In fact, the coincidence of functional stratum (class) and anthroculture (limited to that class), has been frequent in history, occurring whenever conquest or massive migration transplanted members of a given, territorially defined anthroculture to another social system, in which they were to fulfill a specific function. Even if, in the course of time, due to subsequent changes in functional differentiation and attendant mobility, class and anthroculture no longer coincide, the boundary-marking attributes of presentation, communication, and descent—or any of them—may persist. A population group, defined in this manner, and comprising several classes might be termed an *ethnic group*.

The three concepts mentioned here: (a) *anthroculture,* commonly identifying a territorial social system: (b) *socioculture*, as a product of class, and

(c) *ethnic group*, as a social category, sometimes coinciding with class, which within a social system has a recognizable identity of its own based on anthro-cultural attributes (sometimes including descent)—these three concepts seem useful for general analytical purposes (including the analysis of material culture), and *a fortiori* for the study of the three social configurations with which Afro-Caribbean culture is linked, and which in shorthand fashion may be alluded to as that of the African, the slave, and the black.

The slaves waiting for their transportation overseas, and thrown together in African slave-trading ports, came from many African anthrocultures, with languages and religions of their own. A similar situation persisted on the plantations. The rapid mastering of a language in which they could understand themselves and their overseers was a condition for survival. Moreover, it was probably stimulated by psychological impulses produced by the trauma of forced uprooting. In any case the acquisition of a new instrument of social communication must have occurred with incredible speed. Sidney Mintz and Richard Price point appropriately to the absorption, in a few decades after 1667, of the English-influenced Sranang in Surinam by the slaves of Dutch masters.[13] Language, as a vehicle of indispensable social communication, *must* have changed in chameleon fashion with every adaptation to a new territorial system. It is not unthinkable that within a Portuguese port a Portuguese *lingua franca*, on a Dutch slave ship a Dutch *pidgin*, and in a British colony an English-based language, were all learned successively within perhaps a few years. The Creole languages which subsequently evolved in the Caribbean[14] only in rare cases (Aruba, Curaçao, Bonaire) acquired the status of a general vernacular, encompassing the entire population. They did become, however, part of a boundary marking territorial anthroculture— a development which must have been fostered by the fact that the dominant strata in these small islands consisted of linguistically varied groups which, in their mutual contacts, used Papiamentu as a *lingua franca* of their own,[15] thus liberating it from its social stigma. In the British and French colonies (as well as in Surinam) the Creole language remained associated with the lower strata (even though the metropolitan language was subject to creolization). In the Spanish and Portuguese colonies, on the other hand, the creolized metropolitan language became generally adopted, with social and regional variations well within one linguistic span.

It is tempting, as far as the Spanish islands are concerned, to link this linguistic unity to the first phase of slave immigration and the subsequent period of stagnation, which may have encouraged assimilation to the dominant language. Yet, for Brazil this speculation is harder to defend, which leads us to give explanatory force to two other phenomena common to the whole of the Iberian Caribbean: the influence of the Catholic church, and the early formation of a socioracial continuum, both of which, in mutual reinforcement, may have made the boundaries (including the linguistic ones), between the strata more diffuse than was the case in the non-Iberian part of Afro-America.[16] In this latter part, however, the present-day United States would seem to present a curious exception: in spite of its relatively rigid socioracial structure, and notwithstanding some beginnings of a sociolanguage among the slaves and their descendants, no Creole language developed there as encompassing and as distinctive as that in either the British, French, or Dutch islands where it turned into a vehicle which excluded communication with those who only master the metropolitan language. The relatively short period of rapid expansion of North American slave immigration and massive slavery, the relatively small slave numbers per plantation and, finally, the numerical minority position of Afro-Americans in the United States society must have played a significant role here.

Language change, adoption, and invention not only showed a remarkable flexibility (as far as language was used as a vehicle of communication inclusive of the nonslaves), but also a similar linguistic inventiveness was used precisely to restrict communication with outsiders. As a functional stratum, or a class, slaves sometimes fabricated local "secret languages," meant to be unintelligible for masters and overseers. In the communication with the supernatural, use was also made of special "languages" or vocabularies, in which African sounding words and, in the Catholic countries, Latin-derived terms were included.[17] Where slaves or later immigrants from one African language area were able to preserve their language in mutual contact (Cuba, Brazil), speakers of African languages, born in the Western Hemisphere could and can be found.

Religion, as a vehicle for communication with the supernatural, compelled a speedy elaboration of codes, common and distinctive to specific territorially bound systems, be those plantations, regions, or even entire countries. And here, as in language, its flexibility served opposite needs, resulting from the intrinsic ambivalence of the slaves' position. On the one hand, a religion and magic "of their own" as a specific and emotional outlet for the slave population, made for a certain withdrawal from and secretiveness toward the dominant groups. In general, only those religious and magical forms could develop autonomously in slavery that did not rely on advanced specialization and extensive, differentiated organization. The precise contents of these forms, as Melville Herskovits pointed out, often showed similarities between Africa and Europe,[18] which may have stimulated, rather than retarded, their development and expansion in the Western Hemisphere and which makes a detection of their "real" origins an unrealistic undertaking.

On the other hand, there was a need to know about and to participate in the dominant religion. There was pressure on the slaves, exerted by the dominant strata to adhere to Christian churches and beliefs. This pressure was, in a formal sense, most consistent and permanent in the Catholic colonies. It was the (Iberian) Catholic church which, perhaps because of its more universalistic tradition, or its weaker organization at the lower strata level (or a combination of these) showed what in retrospect looks like a greater "tolerance" towards magical and generally "heathen" forms of belief. Whereas the Protestant sects and churches, operating in the British and Dutch colonies and focussing on these strata, generally were stricter in their demands to abandon such practices and beliefs which, consequently, had to go "underground."

In the Protestant colonies, the official metropolitan church showed little interest in converting the slaves. The state church was rather seen as a boundary-marking institution vis-à-vis the lower strata, particularly the slaves, whose Christian salvation was left to either the Catholic church or the smaller Protestant evangelical sects and churches. Where a period of massive slave immigration was followed by a notable weakening of Christian organizations (Haiti), or where massive slave immigration took place in relatively recent times (Cuba, Brazil), the possibilities for organization and specialization, combined with the maintenance of large bodies of African-derived religious beliefs and practices, gave life to clusters of organized, syncretic (but strongly African-influenced) rites, ceremonies, and beliefs. Something similar had, of course, happened earlier in the Maroon communities. The importance of Amerindian influences, including religious ones, on these communities, has perhaps been underestimated. Indeed, generally, the Amerindian contribution to the emergence of creole culture and society in all Caribbean communities where an aboriginal population was present—even though perhaps only in the first, yet crucial, traumatic stage of contact with Europeans and Africans—has so far been underrated.[19]

The above brief notes do not pretend of course, to describe exhaustively the evolution of language, magic, or religion in the Afro-Caribbean environment. They are meant only to suggest that precisely because of their vehicular, group-oriented nature, new language and religious forms and contents could, and had to develop very rapidly, implying a surprising receptivity to whatever was supplied by non-Africans. A speedy "codification" was a necessity for material, social, and spiritual survival.

Such a flexibility also meant the emergence of an immense variety of new linguistic and religious forms and contents in the New World. It has been particularly these new vehicular forms and contents, which have fascinated the classic searchers for "Africanisms," who—as Mintz and Price rightly observe—often tended to interpret the processes by which these new forms and contents came into being, in a rather mechanical way.[20] For our purposes it is important that the adaptive character of these vehicular cultural complexes, of these essential attributes of social and supernatural communication has contributed to the fact that, even where these complexes remained confined to specific functional strata or "classes," they came to distinguish in a marked way these social strata in one Caribbean society from similar strata in the others. It was not a common Caribbean socioculture that emerged. On the contrary, the similar functional strata in the various societies had different anthrocultural characteristics. The similarities that did and do exist on the level of the entire region with respect to language, or the magico-religious field, are "once-removed," determined as they are by whatever common bond there was or is between West African and/or West and South European languages, and between religious and magic representations and practices from these areas. The vehicular forms as they emerged in the Caribbean area are *sui generis* both in their variety and per variety.

It seems to me that a completely different situation exists concerning those nonmaterial African cultural elements, whose reproduction in the New World, unlike the collective vehicles of language and religion, could take place within minimum size (mother-child) units. In particular, I am thinking here of ego-oriented, body-related behavior and activity: of motoric and rhythmic behavior, of facial and corporal gestures, also of the body as a vehicle of transportation, and as an aesthetic object.

The very wide diffusion and similarity of ego- and body-oriented elements over all of Afro-America, their apparent strong resistance to local adaptation and their relative inflexibility, must be understood both in terms of the very early, reflexive type of learning with which these elements are associated, and in terms of a type of behavior and perceptions, common to the different anthrocultures of (Western) Africa. The concept of a Western African "grammar," as suggested by Mintz and Price, comes to mind here, and might be adopted, provided full emphasis is given to the notion of generational transmission.[21]

If one were to denote the culture common to the Afro-American population group as a whole, in terms of unadulterated "Africanisms," these ego- and body-oriented elements should be considered its most important attributes. (This is not to say that all these attributes are still the exclusive property of Afro-Americans; several of them have been adopted, in the course of a creolization process, by other groups in varying breadth and intensity.)

Between the vehicular function of language and religion, and the ego-orientation of the type of behavior that we just mentioned, music, song, and dance occupy an intermediate position. Here, a common "grammar" of motoric and rhythmic elements, mutually recognizable and adoptable

within the Afro-American societies, combines with an impressive variety in
melodic structure in form and in instrumentation, strongly influenced by
non-African traditions and creole innovations, although different in each individual society. It is perhaps this intermediate position with its curious and
unique "blending" which has resulted in a gradual adoption by all strata
and in all Afro-American societies of some music, song, and dance forms. This
distinctive variety per society made them at the same time an important
attribute of each creole anthroculture.

So far, we dealt with "Africanisms": elements from African anthrocultures, and their different degrees of incorporation in the Creole anthrocultures of Afro-America. We now have to direct our attention to the concept of "slave culture" or, broader, to the sociocultures formed predominantly by the slaves and other lower strata in Afro-American societies.
    Criteria of social classification, based on alleged tribal origins, were in wide
use in all slave societies. They were noted in baptismal records and served as
an initial basis for *cofradías* in Catholic societies.[22] The tribal classification
was sometimes even encouraged by the dominant strata or institutions, in
order to divide and rule. Next to these tribal lines of divisions, new group
solidarities came into being, dictated by common function or territorial
position: by the port of disembarkation (Mina slaves); by the ship that transported them (the Cuban *carabelas*), by the degree of experience in the New
World slave system (creoles versus *bozales*); by the nature of slave labor
(house, field, artisanal slaves); by "color" (black, mulatto, etc.), and by legal
status (slave, freedman, freeman). Early on, complementary sets of behavioral
norms for slaves and masters were created which served to assure their complex relationships a modicum of predictability. Outside the narrow confines
of slavery these "slaves" and "masters" patterns of behaviors also made their
influences felt in what was basically, at least initially, a dichotomous hierarchy.[23]
    Mintz and Price point to the frequency and persistence of dyadic, one-
sex, peer relationships (*máti, sippi, malungo, bâtiment*) of which the terms
(shipmate) seem to refer to relations created during the slaves' Atlantic crossing, but the content of which has shifted, e.g., to slaves, working on the same
plantation, or in the case of the Saramaccan *sib* to two persons, victims of
parallel misfortune.[24] We might add that the Surinam *máti* amongst urban
Creoles points to a pair of female homosexuals (also called *kompe*)*, just as
in nineteenth century Curaçao the term *kambrada* (comrade) was reserved
for such partners. The frequency, however, of similar terms in countries with

máti and *kompe* were used among Surinam Bush Negroes to indicate strong friendship
between males.

a strong maritime tradition, such as the Netherlands, makes one inclined to explain their New World incidence not only by referring to the slaves' experience aboard ships, but also to the origin of many members of the incipient dominant social strata: soldiers, sailors, seamen, shipmates, whose vocabulary was well represented in the creolized metropolitan languages, and among whom similar dyadic relationships must have abounded. It would seem to go a bit far, to conclude from the frequency of these terms and relations that they indicated the birth of new societies based on new kinds of principles,[25] especially if one keeps in mind the very special stratum-circumscribed settings which produced them.

Something similar can be said about the frequency of such terms as *bro*, *uncle*, *tio*, *gran* (or the Curaçaoan *swá*–brother-in-law), used to refer to non-relatives of appropriate age. Again, it is hard to see terms as these as specific for New World slaves: the Boers in South Africa were addressed as *oom* (uncle) and *neefie* (little nephew), and, to give one other example, they are still widely in use in certain popular quarters of Amsterdam. The need for such a quasi-kinship terminology seems, in other words, not exclusively linked to a factual weakness of real kinship relations, as the authors suggest,[26] but may generally emerge in small communities or groups, with little internal rank differentiation and with common goals and tasks and a common past. Both the peer dyad and the quasi-kinship terminology were, then, part of the socioculture of slaves and other functional strata, and as such, they were neither "unique," nor could they become a cultural property of Afro-America as a whole, linked as they were and are to specific functional strata.

Family forms, descent rules, and household organizations emerged in considerable variety in the Caribbean, and this variety can only be understood by taking into account differences in demographic, ecological, and economic conditions. The span of this variety may be determined by more durable models derived from Europe or Africa, serving as remote guiding principles or "grammar,"[27] but the variety itself depends on differences in actual position, function, and environment. It is a sociocultural diversity, not an anthrocultural one. In more general terms: "slave" (or "freedman") culture should not be seen as a synonym of Afro-American culture, but rather as the sociocultural product of particular social strata. They do not point to what is common to and distinctive of a culture as a whole, but to its internal cultural diversity arising from functional or ecological differentiation.

At this point, it may be well to remind ourselves of the long period of economic stagnation, occurring in the Spanish islands after the first wave of slave immigration.

It would appear plausible that an absence of demographic injections for a period of at least two centuries and an equally long lasting stability of the

economic system, based predominantly on agrarian subsistence, a low technological level and abundant land resources, must have had consequences for
the manner in which sociocultures were formed and anthrocultural elements
were mutually adopted. In such a stable, subsistence-oriented agrarian system,
without much contact with a monetary economy, cultural artifacts from the
different population groups, related to immediate survival (plants, herbs,
crops, agrarian techniques, construction of dwellings, cooking utensils and re-
cipes, tools, and medicine) were mutually borrowed without much resistance.
The Amerindian contribution (hammock, ceramics, herbal knowledge, fishing, hunting and agrarian techniques, topography) to this exchange must have
been even more impressive than is often, implicitly, assumed. On the other
hand, African and European crops and ways of food preparation, the use of
hoe and machete, or horse and oxen and cattle, all fitted into the general
technological level and were easily and mutually assimilated. The relative
abundance of land during this stagnation period led to a thin and scattered
rural population pattern. The administrative and religious institutions were
far removed from this rural population and without effective influence on
daily life. The boundaries of agrarian land and property were vague, and the
land reserves made formal procedures of inheritance less pressing. The legal
or officially recognized ritual forms of marriage were, therefore, of less importance. Consensus marriages (*amancebados*) were frequent, and the procrea-
tion of descendants with other women was not discouraged. Since land was
not scarce, mechanisms of selection for its monopoly were weakly developed,
and the need for the use of monopolizing pretexts (religion, language, race)
was not great. But there were other systems in the stagnating Spanish colonies
which fitted less well into this pattern.

On the coastal plains sugar *trapiches* keep operating, making slavery functional there. The large numbers of laborers during the cutting season made
for a strict hierarchical system. On the other hand, the extensive cattle
ranches had a much lesser need for labor and the few slaves involved had a
great measure of freedom of movement. Labor relations on ranches were
rather paternalistic. Moreover, since this type of agrarian enterprise, because
of its character, had to be inherited undivided, younger children of the owner
were often given documents representing transferable shares in the holding
(*acciones de pesos*), thus making these *hatos* tantamount to cooperatives with
a large number of members,[28] whose property claims often became hard to
establish in the course of time.

It was perhaps within the urban system that the greatest scarcity of
resources and positions occurred and hence the most forceful efforts were
made toward the definition of group boundaries. Thus, the colonial bureau-
cracy, dependent on external subsidies, was initially bent on reserving its

highest positions for persons born in Spain, a stance, weakened in the course of time by also including "whites" generally, and even "light coloreds." A similar exclusivistic position, with a similar slow widening of the selective criteria, was assumed by the Catholic clergy. Also, the commercial positions, tied closely to governmental favors within the Spanish protectionist system, were predominantly occupied by Spaniards or persons closely related to them.

Throughout the stagnation period this urban system—with its clear and selective allocation of prerogatives, with its cultural and "racial" pretexts for the monopolization of positions and resources, encompassed only a small number of persons, and hardly influenced the much larger system of subsistence farmers. Yet it certainly was the most prestigious due to its direct contacts with the metropolitan agencies. It was also potentially the most influential, incuding as it did the central administrative and religious organizations.

When, in the course of economic change caused by modern, large-scale sugar cultivation, these administrative and religious organizations were able to expand, their higher positions remained primarily the reserve of those persons who qualified on the basis of the earlier developed selective criteria. These criteria also became valid for the higher positions in all other economic sectors where competition for resources and positions prevailed. The remarkable fact was, however, that—compared to the non-Iberian Caribbean colonies—persons who elsewhere would have been defined as (light) "coloreds," and hence mostly excluded from the allocation of high positions (and certainly from marriage with "white" persons from the dominant strata), here often were defined as "white." It is hard to explain this phenomenon purely out of economic and demographic factors, and perhaps we have to refer here to socially determined ideals of beauty, such as those formed during the long Moorish domination in the Iberian Peninsula.[29] This experience partly contributed to the development in the Spanish and Portuguese colonies of a socioracial continuum, compared to what in the Northwest European colonies was generally regarded as a threefold socioracial division (black, colored, white). In contrast, the United States developed a twofold division—(black, white)—accentuated by the exceptionally large number of "poor whites" in that country.

The existence of a socioracial continuum in the Iberian-Caribbean colonies must have facilitated cultural blending and unification especially through language and religion. In this process the numerically important group of "coloreds" served as a social and cultural bridge, or between the ends of the continuum. Where, on the other hand, a socioracial discontinuity existed, the social boundaries between whites and all other groups tended, with rare exceptions, to be reinforced by cultural differences, including language and religion.

On the basis of the foregoing, we might suggest that in the Spanish islands during the period of their stagnation a socioculture of peasants and small farmers was formed, while at the same time within this stratum elements from the anthrocultures of Amerindians, Africans, and Europeans were blended and remolded. These latter elements, not functionally related to the stratum as such, have contributed considerably to the formation of a national, boundary marking creolized anthroculture, thereby elevating music and dance and linguistic peculiarities originating from this stratum such as the Cuban *guajiro*, the Dominican *campesino*, the Puerto Rican *jíbaro*, to the level of national symbols. A comparable process might be observed in Northeastern Brazil, where, however, no clear and long "stagnation period" can be observed. This leads us, again, to attribute a greater relative weight in the process of the formation of national cultural identity in the Iberian countries of Afro-America to the socioracial continuum. Under changing economic conditions, it continued to function as a quasiautonomous force, apparently of longer "duration" than particular economic structures, adding to the cultural contacts between the different "racial" strata another dimension than is the case in the non-Iberian Caribbean. (Where, as in Jamaica, during the nineteenth century and after abolition, a strong peasant stratum developed, a socioculture similar to the early Spanish colonies originated, but its anthrocultural elements remained confined to its own stratum.)

We have now reached the third level on which reflections on the "link" between Africa and the Caribbean can be made. We have dealt with the African anthrocultural influences which, independent of any functional connection to social classes or to the division of labor, spread over the New World. We have already discussed, too, the sociocultural innovations which were the product of particular social strata whose diversity corresponded in large measure to variations in the economic and ecological environment. Now we may evaluate that type of culture which is linked to the African sector originating as a product of this group's broader interrelationship.

We are dealing here, therefore, with culture attitudes, expectations, role behavior, perceptions, the beginnings of group language, ideology, and the formation of common attibutes of descent and presentation, which together define an ethnic group. The social position of this group varied in the different socioracial structures in the Caribbean. Many of these cultural traits developed in a more recent period, outside the assigned scope of this essay. Yet some divergent occurrences were already visible in the eighteenth century.

Of course much earlier—from the first day of contact on, so to speak—there already existed a "we" consciousness of the African group, largely coinciding with that of the slave stratum. But what interests us here is the extent to which such a "we"-feeling maintained, reinforced (over and above the development of functional differentiations within the group of slave origin), and expressed itself. Terms such as *bakra, buckra, macamba*, etc. as early references to the (white) master evolved, it seems, in different societies in the course of their processes of functional differentiation and cultural creolization. They first referred to the white persons in general, and then to the exogenous, or recently arrived, white. In other societies, such as Martinique, the term *beke* kept its original meaning. In Curaçao, a common, territorial, nomer vis-à-vis the colonial outsider only became accepted in this century: *jiu di Korsow* (child of Curaçao). But in a more recent phase of this society's increasing polarization, the internal division is reflected by further differentiating between *bon jiu di Korsow* (good children of Curaçao: the blacks and coloreds), versus *jiu di Korsow* (all others).[30]

In all these societies there exist, of course, terms by which groups distinguish themselves from the "whites,"or between themselves; "people of color" *hende di tristu koló* (people of sad color), "blacks," "mulattos," "Creoles," and "Africans." In the Iberian areas such terms are also frequent, yet it seems to me, based on broad comparative impressions, that here the overt references to one's economic circumstances (*nosotros los pobres*) might be more frequent than those to one's color. The term *blanquitos*, by which certain sectors of the dominant classes are referred to, has a "racial" connotation spiced by the suggestion of racial mixture. Its literal translation (whitey) in the United States, on the other hand, has a completely different and much more antagonistic connotation.

Apparently, it was in the United States that the term "African" was first publicly used as nomer for the black populaton *as a whole*, without reference to any specific functional stratum, by members of that group itself.[31] Associations and churches were given this generic name by persons who, themselves, belonging to the freed or free urban strata, consciously linked their own identity to those of other "Africans" in their country. This remarkable and early (end of the eighteenth century) phenomenon can, as Anani Dzidienyo and Rhett Jones observe, only be understood in terms of the socioracial dichotomy of the United States which offered no "escape" for those who, of mixed ancestry or higher economic position than the slaves and pauperized free people, would always be labeled as "blacks." Thus, they were forced (if they wanted to start social action) to adhere to this dichotomy, using a collective label which transcended internal color and/or class differentiation.

Such an early "dynamic Africanity" in the United States, versus a "frozen Africanity" (the terms are of the authors just mentioned) elsewhere, had no immediate connection with the presence of anthrocultural Africanisms. Such Africanisms, manifest in countries such as Brazil, Haiti, or Cuba, did, and do not imply in the least a strong consciousness of "African" orientation, embedded as they are in anthrocultural elements of different origins, and with a cultural significance in great part derived from their own Creole setting.

Only the "dynamic Africanity" of the Jamaican Rastafari might be an exception here, but probably pertains more to an innovative movement within a given functional stratum than to the impact of anthrocultural "Africanism."

It would seem, then, that the lacks as a conscious and active "ethnic group" developed earliest in the United States because there their functional differentiation was far advanced, yet their society's socioracial structure was least differentiated and most rigid. A similar situation may be observed today in some Caribbean societies (Trinidad, Guyana, Surinam) where an ethnic dichotomy exists (Creoles or "Africans" versus East Indians), where also "Africanity" seems to be more active. An interesting and important subject or speculation is to what extent such a dynamization of blacks as an ethnic group will belatedly occur in other parts of Afro-America, under the influence of an appeal, radiating from North America perhaps more than from Africa, to collective self-consciousness and action.[32] To evaluate this possibility, not only differences in the evolution of socioracial structure must be taken into account, but also the fact that in many Caribbean societies the group in question forms a numerical majority in society. Thus improvements in the position of the black population are simultaneously perceived as structural changes of a national character: national and black emancipation would seem to coincide here.

If this is the case, the role of active guidance, seemingly reserved to the United States because of its "dynamic Africanity" would perhaps be more limited (determined as it is by the numerical minority position of its black population, and by its dichotomous structure) than some would like it to be today.

We have distinguished three types of cultural influence and innovation:

1. The influences from African anthrocultures, blended and molded in the New World, and traditionally labeled "Africanisms," varying from very change-resistant perceptions and behavior of an ego- and body-oriented nature, to vehicles for social and supernatural communication such as language and religion stressing their variety and their diffusion over many functional strata and population groups;

2. Those cultural and social forms of acting and perception, created primarily in the New World as a product of given functional strata and called sociocultures and whose links with Africa or Europe were ephemeral or at least very indirect, and the span of their variety possibly being determined by certain "grammars" common to the cultures of origin. One may think in this respect of slave, peasant, fisherman, and artisan subcultures, or of spatial-social variants such as ghetto culture, or plantation culture; and,

3. Those forms of thought and behavior, created in the New World and most prominent in the United States of America owing to its predominantly creole Afro-American population, and the position which the descendants of the slaves came to occupy as an "ethnic group" within the society at large.

I do not need to emphasize that the different types of culture distinguished here for analytic purposes function in reality as a conglomerate. However, the relative strength of these cultures—and thus the use of the distinctions made—is, it seems to me, crucial for a better understanding of the elusive connection between objectively demonstrable links between Africa and Afro-America, and the subjective significance ascribed to these links by different groupings in different countries at different times.

NOTES

1. José Antonio Saco, *Historia de la esclavitud de la raza africana en el mundo nuevo y en especial en los países américo-hispanos* (Havana, 1938); and Rolando Mellafe, *La introducción de la esclavitud negra en Chile: tráfico y rutas* (Santiago de Chile, 1959), pp. 9-10.

2. For free Africans in Trinidad, see Donald Wood, *Trinidad in Transition* (London, 1968), p. 80; for liberated Africans in the British Virgin Islands, see Isaac Dookhan, "A History of the British Virgini Islands" (Ph.D. diss., University of the West Indies, 1968), pp. 187ff.

3. For Santo Domingo, see Carlos Larrazabal Blanco, *Los negros y la esclavitud en Santo Domingo* (Santo Domingo, 1967), pp. 182ff; for Cuba, see Levi Marrero, *Cuba, economía y sociedad* (Río Piedras, 1972), p. 220.

4. Frank Moya Pons, *La Española en el siglo XVI* (Santiago de los Caballeros, 1971), pp. 243ff.

5. Labor Gomez Acevedo, *Organización y reglamentación del trabajo en el Puerto Rico del siglo 19* (Río Piedras, 1970); also Sidney W. Mintz, *Caribbean Transformations* (Chicago, 1974), pp. 82ff.

6. For a comparison of slavery and race relations between Cuba and Puerto Rico in the nineteenth century, see Franklin W. Knight, *Slave Society in Cuba during the Nineteenth Century* (Madison, Wis., 1970), pp. 179ff.; for a comparison between Puerto

Rico and Jamaica, see Sidney W. Mintz, "Labor and Sugar in Puerto Rico and Jamaica: 1800-1850," *Comparative Studies in Society and History I* (1959): 273-81.

7. Mintz, *Caribbean Transformations*, pp. 180ff.

8. Alan H. Adamson, "The Reconstruction of Plantation Labor after Emancipation: The Case of British Guiana," in *Race and Slavery in the Western Hemisphere: Quantitative Studies*, ed. Stanley L. Engerman and Eugene Genovese (Princeton, 1975), pp. 457-74.

9. Richard Price, ed., *Maroon Societies: Rebel Slave Communities in the Americas* (Garden City, N.Y., 1973); see also, the pertinent bibliographical notes in Franklin W. Knight, *The Caribbean: The Genesis of a Fragmented Nationalism* (New York, 1978), p. 231.

10. Philip D. Curtin, *The Atlantic Slave Trade: A Census* (Madison, Wis., 1969); and "Measuring the Atlantic Slave Trade," in Engerman and Genovese, *Race and Slavery*, pp. 107-29.

11. See, for example, Anani Dzidzienyo, "Afro-Brazilians, Other Afro-Latin Americans, and Africanity: Frozen and Dynamic," unpub. paper, Eighth Annual Meeting, *African Heritage Studies Association*, 1976; and Sidney W. Mintz and Richard Price, *An Anthropological Approach to the Afro-American Past: A Caribbean Perspective* (Philadelphia, 1976).

12. On the concepts of socio- and anthroculture, see also H. Hoetink, "Resource Competition, Monopoly, and Socioracial Diversity," in *Ethnicity and Resource Competition in Plural Societies*, ed. Leo A. Despres (The Hague, 1975), pp. 9-26.

13. Mintz and Price, *An Anthropological Approach*, p. 25.

14. See Dell Hymes, ed., *Pidginization and Creolization of Languages* (New York, 1971).

15. H. Hoetink, *Het patroon van de oude Curaçaose samenleving* (Assen, The Netherlands, 1958), p. 149.

16. See H. Hoetink, *Slavery and Race Relations in the Americas: An Inquiry into Their Nature and Nexus* (New York, 1973).

17. For Curaçao, see Hoetink, *Het patroon*, p. 94.

18. Melville J. Herskovits and Frances S. Herskovits, *Trinidad Village* (New York, 1947), p. 311.

19. For such contacts, however, see Jerome S. Handler, "The Amerindian Slave Population of Barbados in the Seventeenth and Early Eighteenth Centuries," *Caribbean Studies* 8 (1969): 38-64; Douglas N. Taylor, "The Caribs of Dominica," *Smithsonian Institution Bulletin 119: Anthropological Papers*, (1938), pp. 103-60; Jean Hurault, *Africains de Guyane: la vie matérielle et l'art des Noirs refugiés de Guyane* (La Haye, 1970); Richard Price, "Caribbean Fishing and Fishermen: A Historical Sketch," *American Anthropologist* 68 (1966): 1363-84.

20. Mintz and Price, *An Anthropoligical Approach*, p. 7.

21. Ibid, p. 27.

22. For Santo Domingo, see Larrazabal Blanco, *Los negros y la esclavitud*.

23. See Edward Brathwaite, *The Development of Creole Society in Jamaica: 1770-1820* (Oxford, 1971), pp. 176ff.; also Hoetink, *Het patroon*, pp. 124ff.

24. Mintz and Price, *An Anthropological Approach*, pp. 22ff.

25. Ibid., p. 23.

26. Ibid., pp. 37-38.

27. See H. Hoetink, "Formas de organización familiar en el Caribe," *Sonderhefte*, Colegium Humboldtianum (Universität Bielefeld, 1971); Mintz and Price, *An Anthropological Approach*, p. 42.

28. For Santo Domingo, see Antonio del Monte y Tejada, *Historia de Santo Domingo*, 4 vols. (Santo Domingo, 1890), 3:19; for an inspiring appraisal of the role of the

40   HARRY HOETINK

early peasant or yeomen strata in the formation of Hispanic Caribbean nationhood, see Sidney W. Mintz, "Caribbean Nationhood in Anthropological Perspective," in *Caribbean Integration: Papers on Social and Political and Economic Integration*, ed. Sybil Lewis and Thomas G. Mathews (Río Piedras, 1967), pp. 141-55.

29. See Hoetink, *Slavery and Race Relations*, pp. 192ff.

30. R. A. Römer, "Het 'wij' van de Curacaoenaar," *Kristòf*, 1 (1974): 49-61, 53.

31. Rhett S. Jones and Anani Dzidzienyo, "Social Structure and Racial Ideologies in New York," paper, *Conference on the African Mind in the New World*, Rutgers University, 1976, p. 7.

32. Ibid., p. 14.

3

AFRICAN AND CREOLE
SLAVE FAMILY PATTERNS IN TRINIDAD

B. W. Higman

In the study of Caribbean family patterns, few scholars have argued for a genuine continuity of African forms among the black population. Although similarities have been observed between the "matrifocality" of modern Caribbean family structure and the matrilineal systems of particular African groups, it is generally held that this matrifocality can be explained adequately by the slave experience, without reference to the African heritage.[1] Fernando Henriques, for example, contends that the Akan, a matrilineal and polygamous people, were culturally influential in Jamaica but "the direct encouragement of promiscuity by the planters was sufficient to establish a cultural pattern which has persisted to the present day."[2] On the other hand, John and Leatrice MacDonald in their study of Trinidad argue that "matrifocality is a truncated derivative of matrilineages and was a fitting compromise between the African principles of lineage and the new environment, whether or not Negroes passed through slavery."[3] Essentially, most sociologists and historians have adopted a functionalist position, seeing within the period of slavery economic and demographic conditions capable of explaining the family patterns which emerged. These conditions relate particularly to the economic marginalization of the male and the consequently central role of women in the family.

The hypothesis that the African heritage was of minor importance in shaping the family life of West Indian slaves has never been tested rigorously. Nor does the present paper pretend to supply such a test. The necessary data are simply not available. What is attempted here is an examination of the relationship between specific African origins and slave family structures in the island of Trinidad in 1813. This provides a picture of slave family life in the initial stages of the establishment of a plantation economy, the majority of the population being African-born. The changes which took place as Creole (New World-born) slaves became predominant cannot be analyzed systematically.

As Harry Hoetink has indicated in chapter 2, Trinidad was not typical of the sugar colonies of the British Caribbean. It had remained a backwater of the Spanish empire until 1783 when Roman Catholics of any friendly nation were offered free grants of land. The reverberations of the French Revolution in the Antilles made Trinidad a refuge for Francophobes of every color, class, and political persuasion. By the time of the British conquest, in 1797, the population had grown from a mere 1,000 to 18,000, and the flow continued under the British.[4] In 1810, the toal population was about 31,000, 67 percent being slaves, 20 percent freedmen, 8 percent white and 5 percent Amerindian.

This pattern contrasted strongly with that in most of the earlier developed sugar colonies where slaves comprised 90 percent of the population and freedmen only a tiny proportion. A corollary of this contrast was the fact that a large number of slaves in Trinidad belonged to both colored and black freedmen, some of whom were their kin.[5] Equally important for the family patterns of the slaves in Trinidad was their concentration in relatively small holdings, approximating more closely to the distribution found in the United States of America than in the British Caribbean. In Trinidad, 60 percent belonged to units of less than fifty slaves, compared to only 24 percent in Jamaica. Almost 50 percent of Jamaica's slaves were in units of more than 150, and only 8 percent in Trinidad.[6] The relatively small size of slave holdings in Trinidad reflected the relatively heavy urban concentration of the population. In 1813, almost 25 percent of the slaves lived in Port of Spain, whereas in most English Caribbean sugar colonies only 10 percent were employed in towns. Another 20 percent of the Trinidad slaves belonged to holdings producing the minor staples (coffee, cocoa, cotton), so that only a bare majority of them actually lived on sugar estates.

The late acquisition of Trinidad by the English during the agitation against the Atlantic slave trade, and the size of the freedman population, meant that the colony was not granted a legislature similar to those which controlled the slaves in the other British colonies. Rather, Trinidad was made a Crown Colony with all legislation originating in the British Parliament. In theory, the Colonial Office was to maintain firm control over thre free colonists and ensure the amelioration of the conditions under which the slaves lived. Initially, this control was directed toward preventing any illegal continuation of the Atlantic slave trade after it had been abolished by the British in 1807. One means of ensuring this was thought to be the detailed listing of all slaves on the island so that "new" Africans discovered subsequently would be presumed illegally imported. It is this registration of the slaves which provides the basic data for the analysis of family patterns.

An Order in Council proclaimed in Trinidad in 1812 called on every owner of slaves to register them by using standard forms. The forms required the following information about each slave: name, surname, color, employment, age, stature, country (birthplace), bodily marks, family relations.[7] Slaves were grouped into "families" under the surname of the first listed person; and those without relations belonging to the same master were placed in general lists of males and females. The only piece of vital information missing is the sex of the first-listed slaves in families, and this can be established from internal evidence.[8] Most of the registration returns were made in March and April 1813, though a few trickled in as late as December. When the returns had been copied into separate volumes, at the registrar's office in Port of Spain, they were opened for public inspection. Government commissioners then traveled around Trinidad, visiting plantations on the spot, and making occasional corrections to the information supplied by the masters.[9]

In assessing the quality of the registration data it is important to observe that their purpose was the accurate identification of the slaves and that the masters had nothing to gain from falsification. Virtually no contemporary calculations were derived from the data, beyond simple totals, so that they were not consciously manipulated to support any particular thesis. The reported ages display considerable heaping, especially for the Africans, but this stemmed from simple ignorance. The listing of "families" allowed greater latitude for interpretation. Masters were required by the Order in Council to list all slaves who had husbands or wives, "either by actual marriage, or known and constant cohabitation," or who had parents or children, brothers or sisters, among the slaves of the said plantation. Most probably, the "families" approximated family household units, but some of them (juvenile siblings, for example) were no doubt contained within other households while others (adult siblings, for example) were split between units of residence. Thus there was perhaps a tendency to understate the number of extended families. But, in spite of these shortcomings, it remains true that the Trinidad registration data are the most comprehensive available for any West Indian slave population.

The late settlement of Trinidad meant also that at the time of the abolition of the slave trade in 1807 the majority of the slave population had been born in Africa and that few of the African-born had spent more than ten years on the island. It also meant that the regional origins of the Africans

Table 1. Birthplaces of African and Creole Slaves, Trinidad, 1813, and total British
Slave trade, 1791-1800

	Trinidad, 1813			Total British Slave Trade 1791-1800
	Number	(%)	Males per 100 Females	(%)
Africans				
Senegambia	1500	10.7	187	0.7
Sierra Leone	599	4.3	173	4.7
Windward Coast	882	6.3	165	7.5
Gold Coast	1093	7.8	148	13.8
Bight of Benin	1075	7.7	131	1.7
Bight of Biafra	5509	39.4	120	40.5
Central Africa	2555	18.3	173	30.8
Mozambique	11	0.1	300	?
Unidentified	756	5.4	185	?
	13980	100.0	146	100.0
Creoles				
Trinidad	7064	60.7	95	
British colonies	2563	22.0	99	
French colonies	1575	13.5	114	
Spanish colonies	118	1.0	111	
Unidentified	309	2.7	107	
	11629	100.0	99	
African-Creole Unknown	64		427	
TOTAL	25673		122	

SOURCES: T.71/501-503 (Public Record Office, London); and Anstey (1975): 13 (for
1791-1800).
Roger Anstey, "The Volume and Profitability of the British Slave Trade, 1761-
1807," in Stanley L. Engerman and Eugene D. Genovese, eds., *Race and Slavery in
the Western Hemisphere* (Princeton 1975), p. 13.

differed from those typical of populations established in earlier periods.[10]
Trinidad had relatively large proportions from the Bight of Biafra and Central
Africa, and a small proportion from the Guinea Coast (table 1). But Trinidad
also diverged from the regional pattern of the total British slave trade of the
period, receiving an above average number of slaves from Senegambia and the
Bight of Benin, and a relatively small proportion from the Gold Coast and
Central Africa.

These generalizations about the regional origins of the Trinidad African-
born depend on the identification of the "country" names listed in the
registration returns.[11] Some five hundred different labels were used, many
of which cannot be identified with confidence. But with the exception of 134
"Calvers," the unidentified names all apply to small numbers. Most of the
"country" names referred to ethnic groups or tribes, but some described only

shipping points or broad regions, so that a complete breakdown by cultural origin is impossible (table 2). Figure 1 maps the distribution of the major ethnic groups and the shipping points, but omits the broad regional terms. The great geographical spread of the origins of the Trinidad Africans is obvious.

Beyond the problem of identifying the ethnic/regional origins of the African slaves lies the difficulty of establishing the social and cultural patterns existing in their homelands at about 1800. Most of the systematic ethnographic data available date from about 1900 or later, and must be used with caution. Certainly the idea that West Africa formed a unitary culture area, as argued by Melville Herskovits (1941),[12] is no longer acceptable. Such unity should be sought only at the level of values, rather than in concrete sociocultural forms.[13] For an understanding of the family patterns established by slaves in Trinidad, it is important to emphasize the great value placed on kinship by the African societies from which they were taken, and hence the creation of "fictive kin" by slaves lacking real kin in the West Indies.[14] Unilineal descent was also of great importance as an organizing principle, but here the societies divided into those emphasizing patrilineal descent and those emphasizing matrilineal descent. Of the slaves living in Trinidad in 1813 the majority came from patrilineal groups, but the relatively large contingent from Central Africa brought with them the heritage of the matrilineal belt. Matrilineal descent was also important for those from the Gold Coast, and for small pockets of Benin and Biafra.[15] It has been argued that these pockets represent survivals within a general tendency toward patrilineal systems in West Africa; but, whatever the validity of this thesis, it is improbable that a majority of the slaves in Trinidad came from matrilineal soceities.

In Trinidad, the Africans found themselves almost completely cut off from their lineages. A few mothers lived with their African-born children, and a slightly larger number had siblings belonging to the same master. But beyond this the slaves were all isolated individuals, with no common familial norms, or even language, to call on. Further, their transfer dislocated their linking of genealogy and locality, and the veneration of specific pieces of land. Obviously, the full-scale re-creation of any particular African family system was an impossibility. What might be expected, however, is a more subtle differential adaptation of individuals with contrasting African family experiences.

The character of this adaptation must also have reflected the particular circumstances of the African's enslavement. Most of the slaves in Trinidad left Africa before their twentieth year. Thus they must have been taken,

Table 2. Ethnic/Regional Origins of African-Born Slaves, Trinidad, 1813

	Number *of Slaves*
Senegambia	*1500*
Malinke (Mandingo 1416, Mandinga 2, Malinga 1)	1419
Bambara	42
Woloff (Waloff 6, Jaloff 1, Jollof 3)	10
Bram (Bola 2, Bramba 1)	3
Fulbe (Poulard 3)	3
Mayo	1
Wangara (Wanga 1)	1
Diola (Yola 1)	1
Senegal**	15
Gambia**	2
Goree*	2
Coromandel**	1
Sierra Leone	*599*
Fulbe (Foula, Foulah, Fulla, Fuller 171)	171
Susu (Soso, Sosoe, Suso 144, Souci 1)	145
Temne (Trimini, Timmani, Timane, Timene, Timinin, Timipy 148, Temipin 1, Temmana 1, Theminin 3, Tibbeny 3, Timana 1, Timina 1, Timmena 1, Timmni 1, Timna 2, Temana 5, Tamine 1, Tamana 1)	169
Kissi (Kissi, Kissee, Kissy 51, Kiskee 2, Kissa 1, Kissiman 1, Kuisi 1, Quisi 1, Quissi, Quissy 3, Bekissey 1, Qusisy 1, Tisis 1)	63
Bulom (Bolom 1, Bullam 4, Bolonn 1, Bulman, Bullman 2)	8
Koranko (Courango 2, Couwango 1, Curranco 1)	4
Vai (Fye 1, Vea 1)	2
Limba (Limba, Limber 6)	6
Mano (Nana)	1
Mende (Mendé 2, Mendo 1)	3
Ngere (Doo)	3
Kru (Nana)	1
Toma (Tomba)	1
Timbou	5
Kankan [town] (Cancap)	1
Giunea-Bissau** (Portogai 1, Portugas, Portugee, Portugues 12, Portuguese Guina 1)	14
Cape de Verd**	2
Windward Coast	*882*
Kwakwa (Quaqua)	473
Akwa (Aquia 6, Aguia 2)	8
Mesurado hinterland** (Canga 160, Cangar 2, Conga 44, Conger 1)	207
Cape Lahou* (Caplaou 121, Caplahoo, Caplahou 38, Caplahout 1)	160
Windward Coast**	31
Ivory Coast**	3
Gold Coast	*1093*
Bargu (Bargo)	2
Bonda (Bonna)	5
Abron (Bron)	1
Kamana (Camana)	1

Table 2. (*Continued*)

Kokofu (Cocoa)	3
Fanti (Fantee 2, Fonde 1)	3
Akan (Wuaco)	2
Wankyi (Wangwee 3, Wangwing 1)	4
Wassa (Woser)	1
Kormantyn* (Coromantee, Coromanti 354, Caramanti 31)	385
Elmina* (Mine, Minre 283, Mini 14)	297
Anomabu* (Anamabou)	2
Cape Coast castle* (Cape Coast)	2
Gold Coast**	385

Bight of Benin	*1075*
Allada (Arada, Irada 200, Ardda 1, Ladda 1, Rada 78, Raddah 1)	281
Chamba (Chamba 233, Camba 5, Chiamba 1, Cuamba 1, Giamba 1, Jamba 3, Jampa 2, Kiamba 8, Quamba 3, Quiamba 8, Quimba 7, Tiamba 3)	275
Adda (Adda 83, Addé 1, Addo 15)	99
Adja (Adja 6, Aga 5, Agar 1, Aja, Ajah 13, Ajas 1, Ajo 1)	27
Adangme (Ada 10, Ado 37)	47
Agwa (Agra)	1
Hausa (Ahousa, Aousa, Kousa 95, Arousa 1, Ausar 1, Haoussa 1, Hausa 5, Cusa 5, Canaou 1)	109
Ana (Ana 24, Anne 1)	25
Attam (Autan)	2
Bargu (Barba 3)	3
Konkomba (Comba 1, Combah 2)	3
Kumba (Cumba)	1
Dian (Dya)	2
Edo (Eddo)	1
Wara (Guala)	3
Manga	1
Ge (Mina, Minna)	33
Munga	1
Yoruba (Nago)	8
Popo (Papa 104, Papaw 2, Pappa 5, Pawpau 1)	112
Whydah (Whadah 1, Wydan 1)	2
Yoruba (Yolaba 1, Yruba 1)	2
Apa* (Apa 5, Appa 9, Apay 1)	15
Dahomey** (Dahomet 1, Dahomin 1)	2
Slave Coast**	20

Bight of Biafra	*5509*
Igbo (Ibo 2727, Ebo 134)	2861
Northwestern Bantu (Moco 2233, Moko 1)	2234
Ibibio (Bibi 364, Bibe 1, Ibibia 3)	368
Ijaw (Aijo)	1
Anang (Anan)	4
Bana (Bahna)	1
Banda	1
Banggolo (Bangolo)	1
Baji (Bolo)	1
Holma (Homa)	1

Table 2. *(Continued)*

Lumbo (Lumba)	5
Wawa	1
Bonny* (Bonny 4, Bonni 1)	5
Calabar* (Calabar 19, Calabay 1, Caravali 1)	21
Gaboon**	4
Central Africa	*2555*
Kongo (Congo 2448, Gongo 1)	2449
Bachoko (Bacoco)	1
Ngala (Bangala, Bangara 3)	3
Ekonda (Baseca)	1
Kutshu (Bolono)	1
Kasai (Bundu)	2
Cabinda (Cabonda)	1
Eton (Etton)	1
Hamba (Hamba)	2
Vili (Loango 1, Vihi 4)	5
Mondonga (Mondongue)	3
Kwese (Quesa)	1
Samba	7
Soko (Soko 1, Socko 15, Soco 1)	17
Sorongo (Solongo)	2
Angola**	59
Mozambique	*11*
Yao (Ayo 1)	1
Nguni ? (Caffre)	1
Makoa (Macoua)	1
Mozambique**	8
Unidentified	*523*
Adow	5
Anooba	6
Auca	5
Bouriqui	5
Bruckum	5
Calbe	5
Calver	134
Chique	9
Gruma	5
Morocco	6
Ossa	5
Succo	13
Others (less than five slaves each)	320
Africans (so described)	233

NOTE: Names in parentheses are the labels found in the registration returns. The numbers give their frequency. These are proceded by an ethnic/tribal identification.
* indicates a shipping point.
** indicates a geographic region.
SOURCE: T. 71/501-503.

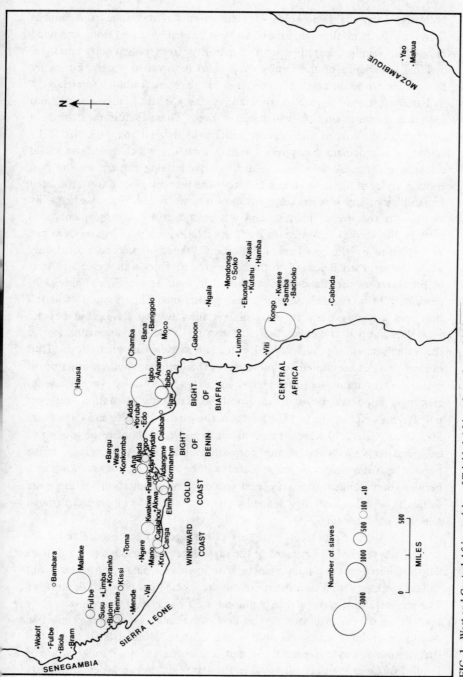

FIG. 1. West and Central Africa: origins of Trinidad African-born slaves, 1813.

typically, from the households of their parents rather than from families founded by them through marriage. Most probably came from extended or nuclear families, together with a minority from polygynous units. In- dividual experience of the family cycle must have varied widely, but many slaves were no doubt taken at some point in the rituals leading to marriage.[16]

Family patterns were also affected by the specific kinds of social and economic environments in which slaves lived. These factors must be held constant if the role of the African heritage in familial adaptation is to be traced. In particular, the types of family structure which the slaves could establish in Trinidad were determined by slave-holding size and by the con- trasting styles of life in town and country. The percentage of slaves attributed to families of any sort in the registration returns of 1813 increased steadily along with the size of holding, and was always greater on the plantations than in the towns (figure 2). In part, the relationship with holding size can be explained by the problem of definition: "families" were identified only when the members belonged to the same master. Thus, although 50 percent of the slaves on the island were attributed to families overall, as many as 74 percent were in families on the largest plantations. The question of defini- tion was probably basic in units of less than twenty slaves, but beyond that size group it is evident that size also meant greater opportunities for the establishment of nuclear and extended families on plantations. Thus nuclear families accounted for more slaves than mother-children units on all plantations of more than fifty slaves, and extended families also became in- creasingly important beyond that threshold. The only plantation to report polygynous units was in fact the largest in the island—Paradise and Cane Farm Plantation, with 250 slaves. Large plantations were relatively permissive to extended and polygynous family formation because they provided a larger population from which to choose mates (without breaking rules of exogamy), because they tended to be isolated (making cross-plantation mating more difficult), and because they tended to be less subject to separation through sale than small holdings.

In the towns 61 percent of the slaves belonged to holdings of ten slaves or less, whereas only 15 percent of the rural slaves were in such units. But the contrast between the family structure of town and plantation slaves is not to be explained simply as a function of holding-size (and hence of definition). The proportion of slaves living in nuclear units was always much lower in the towns than on the plantations, regardless of holding size, and the proportion of mother-children units was always much larger. More striking is the fact that in the towns the proportion not attributed to any family grouping levelled out and then actually rose as the slave-holdings grew beyond twenty

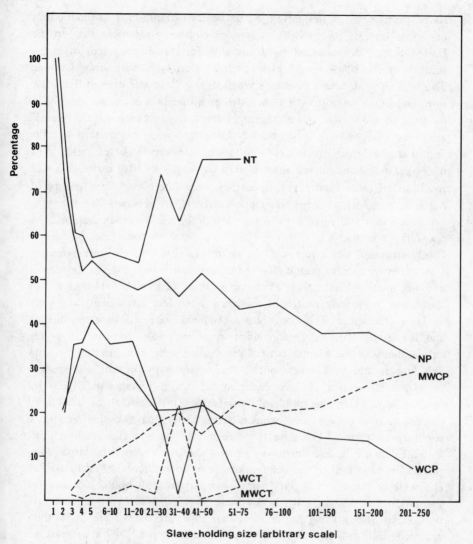

FIG. 2. Percentage of slaves in select family types by slave-holding size: Trinidad, 1813.

Key: NT   No family (town).
      NP   No family (plantation).
      WCT   Woman-children (town).
      WCP   Woman-children (plantation).
      MWCT Man-wife-children (town).
      MWCP Man-wife-children (plantation).

slaves, diverging from the pattern on plantations (figure 2). This finding is of particular interest in the light of Herbert Gutman's argument that, in the United States, urbanization is accountable for the development of matri-focality in the black family *after* emancipation (especially since Gutman does not present data on urban slave families).[17] In the case of Trinidad, it is important to notice that the African proportion increased sharply in holdings of more than twenty slaves in the towns, whereas on the planta-tions the increase was very gradual. Associated with this pattern was the fact that the larger urban units tended to have very high sex ratios (214 males per one hundred females for units of twenty to fifty males, and 422 for units of more than fifty), since they were often specialized groups of builders, quarriers, limemakers, tanners, bakers, or seamen. Yet the Afri-can proportion tended to be relatively low in the smaller urban units and the sex ratio was also low. Thus the contrast between town and plantation family structure was a real one, the towns permitting much more extensive mating between slaves with different masters, and between slaves and whites and freedmen. Whereas there is strong evidence of kinship networks within the towns, they were rooted in residence much less often than they were on large plantations. The towns also engendered occupational independence and hence the economic marginalization of the male, to a much greater extent than did the plantations (where women were concentrated into the field gangs, and men monopolized the occupations of skill and status).

Of the 50 percent of slaves living in families in Trinidad in 1813, 44.2 percent were in mother-children units (table 3). Almost all of the family units were of this type, most women having fewer than two children. But a similar proportion of the slaves lived in nuclear or truncated nuclear units, including man-wife and "man-wife-various children" types (the latter com-prising combinations of the children of one or both parents).[18] Although the character of the Trinidad data makes comparison with household data for plantation Jamaica difficult, it is evident that Trinidad had a smaller pro-portion of slaves living in families, that more of them were in mother-centered units and that fewer lived in extended types.[19] This contrast re-sulted chiefly from the relatively large urban and African-born components in the Trinidad population.

The contrast between African and creole family patterns in both town and country is understood more readily if slaves under fifteen years of age are excluded from the analysis, since most of them were creoles by 1813, and few played any active part in family formation. In the first place, it is clear that mother-children families predominated overwhelmingly in the towns among both African and creoles. (It is important to notice that this urban

Table 3. Slave Family Types, Trinidad, 1813

Family Type	Family Units	Slaves	Mean Size	Slaves in families (%) Units	(%) Slaves
Man, wife, their children	932	3670	3.9	22.3	28.5
Man, wife	518	1036	2.0	12.4	8.1
Woman, her children	2066	5690	2.8	49.4	44.2
Man, his children	138	357	2.6	3.3	2.8
Woman, her children, her grandchildren	48	227	4.7	1.1	1.8
Man, wife, various children	230	1005	4.4	5.5	7.8
Polygynists	7	31	4.4	0.2	0.2
Extended	49	218	4.4	1.2	1.7
Siblings, and their children	197	547	2.8	4.7	4.2
Total in families	4185	12781	3.1		50.1
Slaves not in families		12892			49.9
TOTAL		25673			100.0

SOURCE: T.71/501-503.

pattern may be at the root of the traditional interpretation of the "matri-focal" slave family; most contemporary white observers knew more about the towns than the plantation villages, and learned more from their cooks than from their field hands.) But when, in the towns, slaves managed to establish nuclear families, it was the Africans who most frequently founded them. Some 17.8 percent of the urban Africans lived in nuclear or truncated nuclear families (as defined above), but only 5.6 percent of the urban creoles. As noted earlier, this contrast cannot be explained by the concentration of Africans in the larger urban slave holdings. It may be that the creoles, circulating more confidently, were more likely to find mates belonging to other masters but such unions must often have lacked a coresidential basis, necessarily making them looser relationships.

On the plantations, the contrast between African and creole family structure was equally strong (table 4). Africans were less likely to find themselves in families than were creoles, as in the towns.[20] But, of the slaves who were in families, once again it was the creoles who were dominated by mother-centered units while Africans were twice as frequently to be found in nuclear units. Otherwise, only in those family types which depended on generational depth did the creoles, inevitably, predominate. Thus, extended families,

54   B. W. HIGMAN

Table 4. Percentage of African and Creole Slaves Fifteen Years and over, by Family
          Type, Trinidad, 1813

| Family Type | Slaves Living in Families | | | | |
| | Plantation | | Town | | |
	African	Creole	African	Creole	Total
Man, wife, their children	40.2	20.3	11.4	2.9	29.1
Man, wife	22.6	7.1	3.4	1.1	14.8
Woman, her children	22.8	42.7	78.9	73.0	37.1
Man, his children	2.6	4.2	1.3	0.7	2.8
Woman, her children, her grandchildren	0.7	4.0	0.6	3.9	1.9
Man, wife, various children	9.3	7.3	3.0	1.6	7.6
Polygynists	0.5	0.1	0.0	0.0	0.3
Extended	1.0	5.0	0.0	0.4	2.0
Siblings, and their children	0.3	9.3	1.3	16.5	4.7
	100.0	100.0	100.0	100.0	100.0
Number in families	3800	2095	527	559	6981
Number not in families	6923	1563	2523	963	11972
Percent not in families	64.6	42.7	82.7	63.3	63.2

SOURCE: T. 71/501-503.

grandmother-centered families and groups of siblings (resulting from separation of parents by sale or death) were all comprised largely of creoles. But
creoles were less likely to belong to polygynous families. Overall, Africans
were much more likely to live in families containing mates than were creoles.
This applies even if slaves without families are included in the calculation, in
both town and country. On the plantations, 26 percent of the slaves fifteen
years and over lived in families containing mates but only 22 percent of the
creoles (the calculation being weighted in favor of the creoles, since a proportion of them were children in units headed by Africans).

It seems clear, then, that the African-born were more successful than the
creoles in establishing families centered on co-resident mates, independent
of the circumstances in which they found themselves. The nuclear family,
of course, was not traditionally normative for any of the Trinidad Africans,
with the exception of the matrilineal Kongo.[21] It must have been seen by
most of the African-born merely as the essential building block of extended
or polygynous family types rooted in lineage and locality. Their creole

descendants, however, either lost sight of these models (as a part of the process of creolization) or were prevented from achieving them by the brutality of the slave regime (heavy mortality, separation by sale, miscegenation, Christian proselytism, and so on).

Africans with different ethnic/regional origins were always mixed together on individual plantations. In part this resulted from a conscious attempt by the masters to control their slaves by inhibiting communication and solidarity. It also derived from the purchasing of small groups of slaves from single slave ships, so that the masters were unable to build up a homogeneous population even though expressing strong preferences for particular tribal groups.[22] The Africans themselves shared prejudices against other groups, and generally preferred to form families with those who shared a common culture and language. Obviously, those who belonged to the largest contingents were likely to have most success in finding partners. Thus the percentage of Africans who lacked family links was closely related to the number of slaves drawn from a common region (table 5).

Most of the Africans in Trinidad who were successful in finding mates found Africans. Of the African males with wives in 1813 only 10 percent had creole mates. Of the African females with husbands, 13 percent had creole mates. Thus, even though there was a preponderance of African-born males in the population, creole men were able to compete successfully for African women. Among the Africans themselves, there was a considerable mating between those from different regions (table 6). Of those Africans who did have mates (belonging to the same owner) only 32 percent found partners from their own region. The extent of regional endogamy was closely related to the size of the contingent. Thus, no slaves from Sierra Leone, the smallest of the regional contingents, found mates among their fellows. On the other hand, 65 percent of males from the Bight of Biafra had wives from the same region.[23] With the exception of those from the Bight of Biafra, African women were always more endogamous, regionally, than the men. In terms of familial models, it is not clear that those Africans who mated outside their region showed any preference for partners with compatible heritages. For example, males from Central Africa and the Gold Coast, regions with matrilineal traditions, more often found wives from the patrilineal Bight of Biafra than from their own regions. But the women of Central Africa and the Gold Coast were more selective, the largest number of their mates coming from the same region.

In addition to the effect of the absolute size of the tribal/regional contingent, the extent of regional endogamy was also related to the sex ratios of the particular African groups. These sex ratios varied regionally much more

Table 5. Family Types of African Regional Groups, Trinidad, 1813

	Percentage of Slaves in Families						
Family Type	Senegambia	Sierra Leone	Windward Coast	Gold Coast	Bight of Benin	Bight of Biafra	Central Africa
Man, wife, their children	34.0	44.2	36.6	31.6	36.2	39.0	33.0
Man, wife	24.2	13.7	19.5	18.4	19.1	18.1	24.7
Woman, her children	27.0	25.3	29.8	34.9	25.9	30.9	28.6
Man, his children	2.3	1.1	3.8	2.0	2.0	2.2	2.7
Woman, her children, her grandchildren	0.5	0.0	0.8	0.6	0.9	0.9	0.4
Man, wife, various children	9.9	14.7	9.5	10.1	11.7	7.6	8.6
Polygynists	0.2	0.0	0.0	0.0	0.6	0.6	0.9
Extended	1.9	1.1	0.0	0.6	2.0	0.6	1.1
Siblings, and their children	0.0	0.0	0.0	2.0	1.7	0.1	0.0
	100.0	100.0	100.0	100.0	100.0	100.0	100.0
Percentage not in families	71.1	71.5	70.9	68.4	62.7	67.5	70.6

SOURCE: T.71/501-503.

Table 6. Regional Origins of African Mates, Trinidad, 1813

Husband's Regions:	Wife's Region:								
	Senegambia	Sierra Leone	Windward Coast	Gold Coast	Bight of Benin	Bight of Biafra	Central Africa	Creoles	Total
Senegambia	33	3	8	11	16	58	19	19	167
Sierra Leone	3	0	2	2	6	14	5	6	38
Windward Coast	9	0	18	7	7	29	9	17	96
Gold Coast	7	5	4	25	10	34	11	13	109
Bight of Benin	4	3	6	1	17	42	27	14	114
Bight of Biafra	24	4	14	23	17	303	52	28	465
Central Africa	11	4	8	10	12	90	80	22	237
Creoles	12	4	9	16	19	76	30	106	272
TOTAL	103	23	69	95	104	646	233	225	1498

SOURCE: T.71/501-503.
NOTE: Excludes those whose region could not be identified.

than might have been expected. They ranged from 187 males per 100 females for Senegambia to 120 for the Bight of Biafra (Table 1). Thus the relatively low sex ratio for slaves from the Bight of Biafra may account for those two features noted earlier, the high proportion of males having mates from their own region and the tendency for women from Biafra to mate widely with men of other regions. As a corollary, Africans tended more often to live in families the closer the sex ratio came to 100. Nuclear families tended to be more common the lower the sex ratio, but this relationship was not very strong.

Taking together the effects of variations in the size of African regional contingents and in their sex ratios, it must be concluded that the amount of genuine variation in family structure between the different regional groups was not great. This conclusion is not surprising, of course. But it must be tempered somewhat if the focus is shifted from the region to the ethnic group or tribe, that is, to slaves attributed by the masters to a single named origin ("country"). This minimizes the problem of identification error and cultural heterogeneity. It has been observed already that although the masters used about 500 names in describing the origins of the Trinidad Africans, eleven of these account for 79 percent of the total (Ibo, Moco, Congo, Quaqua, Gold Coast, Coromantee, Mine, Mandingo, Bibi, Chamba, Arada). Of these eleven groups, one stands out clearly from the rest in terms of family structure—the Igbo (Ibo).

The Igbo (the major component of the Bight of Biafra regional grouping) were distinguished principally by their participation in family units based on generational depth, extension, and polygyny. This applied in both town and country. Taking these types of families together, they are found to contain thirty-two Igbo and only thirty-nine of the other major African groups; that is, the Igbo lived in such units more than twice as frequently as the other Africans (1.2 percent of the Igbo, compared to 0.5 percent of the others). Again, the Igbo had the largest proportion living in nuclear families (20.5 percent), potential bases for extension and polygyny. The Igbo in Africa lived in large extended families, grouped in fairly small dispersed hamlets, but regarded polygyny as the ideal family form (a symbol of status, attained by only the few). They practised lineage exogamy, prohibiting the marriage of first and second cousins. Marriage was patrilocal.[24] It is obvious that not all of these features could function in Trinidad under slavery, but the structural similarity of the two familial patterns remains striking.

The large extended family occupying a compound was not unique to the Igbo as a familial norm. So the relative success of the Igbo in re-creating their African family system in Trinidad under the conditions of slavery must be attributed to their absolute number (2,200) and their low sex ratio. Similarly, the relative failure of the Malinke (Mandingo), who held similar familial ideals and comprised a considerable contingent in Trinidad (1,098), must be explained by their high sex ratio. Thus it must be concluded that the demographic selectivity of the slave trade determined very largely the extent to which particular groups of Africans could fulfill their familial ideals or norms. It is, however, equally important to notice that when the demographic conditions *were* relatively favorable, as in the case of the Igbo, slaves did establish a variety of family forms, reflecting in some measure their particular African cultural heritage. Such favorable conditions were simply a great rarity.

The analysis thus far has been essentially structural. Little has been said of the quality of the familial relationships in the various types of units or of the principles which controlled their formation and dissolution. It is obvious that the functions of the family and household in Africa differed dramatically from those performed under New World slavery. It must therefore be asked to what extent slaves living in families structurally similar to those of their African cultures perceived their place in them as functionally and emotionally similar. Unfortunately, it is impossible to give satisfying answers to these questions because of the limitations of the available data. But indirect approaches can be tried.

To begin, it has sometimes been argued that the supposed economic marginalization of the slave male meant that households which were nuclear in structure were essentially matrifocal in function. One way of testing this proposition is to consider the occupations of the male heads of such units. (Only two nuclear units were listed in the Trinidad registration returns with the wife placed ahead of the husband, but this ordering might be explained by the cultural forms of the masters.) Only about 60 percent of the male heads of nuclear families were laborers, compared to 90 percent of their wives. At least one-third of the male heads were skilled tradesmen or drivers, positions of status within the slave hierarchy carrying with them material rewards and opportunities. Among the polygynists, as many as 60 percent of the male heads were skilled, while all of their wives were laborers. This pattern suggests that the values given to the headship of nuclear and polygynous families in Africa did not disappear entirely in Trinidad slave society. It is also important to observe that the allocation of tasks by sex under slavery was compatible with the predominant role of women in agricultural labor in the major African societies from which the slaves came. Certainly, the male head of a nuclear or polygynous family in Trinidad could not perform all of his traditional roles under slavery, but it seems equally unlikely that he surrendered them to the wife while retaining his relative economic status. In mother-children families there were as many domestics as laborers among the heads, a corollary of their urban concentration.

From the child's perspective, it is important to notice that overall the majority lived in families headed by their mothers. In 1813 some 3,783 children lived with their mothers only, while 2,003 were with both parents and 352 lived with mates only one of whom (most often the mother) was their parent. Although it is difficult to assess the impact of mortality on this pattern, and recognizing the contrasting experience of children of African and creole parentage, it is obvious that the potential for matrifocal development was great so long as the urban concentration of the slave population continued.

Since the Trinidad data are essentially only a census, it is impossible to trace the family through its development cycle or to measure its stability. But the distribution of women among the different family types by age does not suggest that they only settled with mates in later life, after bearing children. Rather, the matrifocal and nuclear family types were alternatives from the beginning, as in modern family structure.[25] Thus many women had children by men with whom they never lived, a condition directly related to the slave system but not necessarily evidence of "instability." Although the data must be approached with caution, it is singificant that of the 3,535 slave "offenses" reported by the Trinidad Protectors of Slaves in 1827-28 only three men were accused of "seducing, and attempting to seduce, other men's wives" and two women with "infidelity to husband."[26] Another three men were accused of rape and three women of "fornication." Thus, although quarrels and violence were common in the slave quarters, infidelity seems rarely to have been a causative factor. But slavery meant that instability resulting from mortality and separation could exist alongside social sanctions against it within the slave community; and it is extremely difficult to disentangle these alternative interpretations from the data.

The role of parents in the choice of mates for their children is very uncertain. There is no definite evidence of a prohibition on cousin marriage as argued for the United States by Gutman.[27] Indeed, the one piece of relevant West Indian folklore is contradictory. A Jamaican proverb, first collected in the later nineteenth century, runs "cousin boil sweet soup," meaning that "although second cousins should not marry, a match between first cousins is considered especially desirable."[28] Again, there is no evidence of the practice of bridewealth in the West Indies, one of the universal features of West African marriage. If it was in fact absent, this suggests a very considerable loosening in the role of parents in the choice of marriage partners. The survival of the institution was in jeopardy, of course, simply because the African-born slaves did not have parents to receive bridewealth, however symbolic. Unlike the situation found in the United States, there is no evidence of any form of ceremony validating slave marriage (other than Christian marriage) and only weak evidence of a ritual connected with divorce.[29]

Attitudes to children are also poorly understood. In 1827-28 the Trinidad Protectors of Slaves reported that only two men and three women had been accused of "maltreating children."[30] On the other hand, Patterson has argued that Jamaican slave mothers treated their children with a mixture of "extreme cruelty and great love and affection."[31] But it is at least clear that children regarded their parents with veneration.

No detailed study of slave-naming patterns has yet been made for the West Indies, and it is doubtful how much is to be learned from any analysis restricted to the master-approved names recorded in lists such as the Trinidad registration returns.[32] The surnames attributed to the slaves in 1813 seem largely to have been imposed by the masters, employing their own "aesthetics of play and creativity," but probably having little currency among the slaves. In plantation Trinidad, sons were more likely to be given their father's name than daughters their mother's, as observed in the United States.[33] But in Port of Spain this distinction was absent.[34] There was no contrast between African and creoles in this behavior. Some daughters seem to have been named after their mother's sisters or their grandmothers, but the 1813 census lacks sufficient generational depth to test the frequency of this pattern.

There is quite strong evidence that West Indian slaves maintained the custom widespread in West Africa, of prolonged breast feeding, in the face of opposition from the masters. Slave mothers frequently delayed weaning for more than two years, so that spacing of births was relatively wide.[35] Whether this delay was practiced by both Africans and creoles is uncertain. It is also unknown whether women abstained from sexual intercourse during this period of breast feeding (as in Africa), or whether the continued lactation alone had sufficient contraceptive effect to account for the wide spacing of births. The fact that the masters actively opposed this custom, chiefly because it reduced the amount of time spent in field labor but also because it inhibited reproduction, meant that its continuance was in itself an act of resistance. But it must also be seen as strong evidence of the bond between mother and child, a bond which existed (as in Africa) in all types of family structure, not only in those which were matrifocal.

It should be clear from these few observations that the available evidence does not permit a full understanding of the functioning and emotional life of the slave family. The only systematic data are those that *describe* structure, thus it is necessary to use these as the framework for any wider analysis. This, admittedly, is a severe limitation. Yet several conclusions do emerge quite strongly from this study of Trinidad.

1. The majority of African-born slaves in a newly settled plantation society were isolated from any formal family system.

2. Distinct African ethnic/tribal groups lost their identity almost immediately, as a result of extensive intermarriage. Only those groups which constituted a substantial proportion of the total slave population, and had a relatively natural sex ratio, were able to establish family patterns which reflected however vaguely their particular culture history.

3. Families established by Africans contrasted strongly with those of creoles. It is not true to say that Africans had no option but to fall in with the creole pattern, at least in those societies which contained a large proportion of African-born slaves.[36]

4. A matrifocal tendency in family structure can be discerned as the creole population grew, but it is not clear how far this tendency affected familial norms and ideals. For the children of Africans the norm remained the extended family, but the difficulty of achieving this outside of large stable plantations meant that the nuclear family was predominant in most rural areas and the mother-child unit in towns.

NOTES

I thank Franklin Knight for encouraging me to write this essay for presentation at the Houston meeting of the Latin American Studies Association in November 1977. As well as commenting on an early draft, Stanley Engerman generously permitted me to use his tape of the first 5,000 plantation slaves from the Trinidad registration returns, for which I thank him. I have partially recoded this sample and repunched it in order to ensure consistency within the total data-set. The original version of this essay was published in the *Journal of Family History* (Summer 1978) and is reprinted with the permission of the editors.

1. Hyman Rodman, *Lower Class Families: The Culture of Poverty in Negro Trinidad* (London, 1971), p. 8.

2. Fernando Henriques, *Family and Colour in Jamaica* (London, 1953).

3. John S. MacDonald and Leatrice D. MacDonald, "Transformation of African and Indian Family Traditions in the South Caribbean," *Comparative Studies in Society and History* 15 (1973): 171-98.

4. James Millette, *The Genesis of Crown Colony Government: Trinidad 1783-1810* (Curepe, Trinidad, 1970).

5. The masters were rarely identified by color or status in the list of slave families used here, so it is impossible to test their significance.

6. Barry W. Higman, *Slave Population and Economy in Jamaica, 1807-1834* (Cambridge, 1976).

7. British Colonial Office 295/28 folio 250. (Public Record Office, London, 1812).

8. Sex can generally be inferred from the family relationships, occupation, and/or name. Where individuals with ambiguous occupations and names were simply the parents of children, they have been assumed to be female. The sex of siblings cannot be assumed, and in cases of ambiguity the most probable interpretation of the name has been used.

9. Great Britain, *Parliamentary Papers* 16 (1823): 76.

9. Great Britain, *Parliamentary Papers* 16 (1823): 76.

10. Philip D. Curtin, *The Atlantic Slave Trade: A Census* (Madison, Wis., 1969).

11. The identifications are based chiefly on material in George P. Murdock, *Africa: Its People and Their Cultural History* (New York, 1959); and Curtin, *Atlantic Slave Trade*. I am grateful to Philip Curtin and Roberta Kilkenny for their help in making these identifications.

12. Melville J. Herskovits, *The Myth of the Negro Past* (Boston, 1941).

13. Sidney W. Mintz and Richard Price, *An Anthropological Approach to the Afro-American Past: A Caribbean Perspective* (Philadelphia, 1976), p. 5.

14. Orlando Patterson, "From Endo-deme to Matri-deme: An Interpretation of the Development of Kinship and Social Organization Among the Slaves of Jamaica, 1655-1830," in *Eighteenth Century Florida and the Caribbean*, ed. Samuel Proctor (Gainesville, Fla., 1976).

15. Murdock, *Africa*, p. 28; and Philip O. Nsugbe, *Ohaffia: A Matrilineal Ibo People* (Oxford, 1974).

16. Arthur Phillips, ed., *Survey of African Marriage and Family Life* (London, 1953).

17. Herbert G. Gutman, *The Black Family in Slavery and Freedom, 1750-1925* (New York, 1976).

18. The pattern in Table 3, for the entire Trinidad slave population, can be compared with that reported for a sample comprising the first 1,296 plantation slaves listed in the registration returns (Higman, *Slave Population*, p. 266). That sample contained the largest plantation in the island (250 slaves) and excluded all "personal" slaves. It greatly overestimated the number of polygymous (4.5 percent of the slaves), extended (6.4), and man-wife (16.1) families, and underestimated women-children (27.2) and man-wife-various children (2.6) units. The dangers of nonrandom sampling of census lists are obvious.

19. Barry W. Higman, "Household Structure and Fertility on Jamaican Slave Plantations: A Nineteenth Century Example," *Population Studies* 27 (1973): 527-50.

20. Of the population fifteen years and over, 74.6 percent were African-born on the plantations and 66.7 percent in the towns.

21. Murdock, *Africa*; and Georges Balandier, *La vie quotidienne au royaume de Kongo du XVIe au XVIIIe siècles* (Paris, 1965).

22. Orlando Patterson, *The Sociology of Slavery: An Analysis of the Origins, Development, and Structure of Negro Slave Society in Jamaica* (London, 1967); Monica Schuler, "Ethnic Slave Rebellions in the Caribbean and the Guianas," *Journal of Social History* 3, no. 4 (1970): 474-85; and idem, "Akan Slave Rebellions in the British Caribbean," *Savacou* 1, no. 1 (June 1970): 8-31.

23. Note that Curtin, *Atlantic Slave Trade*, p. 188, describes the "Moco" as "a diverse range of peoples and cultures shipped from slave ports on the lower Cross River." Thus the Bight of Biafra region contained within it significant cultural diversity.

24. Edwin Ardener, "Lineage and Locality among the Mba-Ise-Ibo," *Africa*, 29 (1959): 113-33; Victor C. Uchenda, *The Igbo of Southeastern Nigeria* (New York, 1965); Elizabeth Isichei, *A History of the Ibo People* (New York, 1976); Sylvia Leith-Ross, *African Women: A Study of the Ibo of Nigeria* (London, 1939); and Olaudah Equiano, *Equiano's Travels: The Interesting Life of Olaudah Equiano, or Gustavus Vassa, the African* (London, 1789).

25. Hymie Rubenstein, "Diachronic Inference and the Pattern of Lower Class Afro-Caribbean Marriage," *Social and Economic Studies* 26 (1977): 202-16.

26. The most common "offences" reported were "neglect of duty" (852 cases), "absconding, running away" (516), and "theft" (207). Another 193 slaves were charged with quarreling, fighting, beating, biting, scalding, or cutting with cutlasses (P. P. 1830-1:340). Only one man seems to have been convicted of raping a slave, a virgin, thirteen years old (P. P. 1830-1:333). Overall, it is uncertain how many of the accusations came from the masters and how many from the slaves.

27. Gutman, *Black Family*, passim.

28. Martha W. Beckwith, *Jamaica Folk-Lore* (New York, 1928).

29. Patterson, *Sociology*, p. 162.

30. Great Britain, *Parliamentary Papers, 1830-31* (262), Protector of Slaves Reports, p. 340.

31. Patterson, *Sociology*, p. 168.

32. Richard Price and Sally Price, "Saramaka Onomastics: An Afro-American Naming System," *Ethnology* 11 (1972): 341-67.

33. Gutman, *Black Family*, p. 190.

34. The plantation sample comprised 188 mothers with surviving daughters and 121 fathers with sons, only two of the latter giving their sons their first names (T.71/501, folios 1-100, Public Record Office, London). For Port of Spain: 221 mothers with daughters, nine having the same name; twenty one fathers with sons, two having the same name (T.71/503, folios 1-79 and 392-632). Only exact correspondences were counted.

35. Herbert S. Klein and Stanley Engerman, "Fertility Differentials Between Slaves in the United States and the British West Indies: A Note on Lactation Practices and Their Possible Implications," *William and Mary Quarterly*, Third Series, 35, no. 2. (April 1978): 357-74.

36. For a contrary view, see Patterson, *Sociology*, p. 159.

4

MYALISM AND THE AFRICAN
RELIGIOUS TRADITION IN JAMAICA

Monica Schuler

Religious movements have played a central role in Jamaican history for three centuries. Impossible to ignore, they have proved difficult to understand because scholars have tended to interpret them primarily as the frustrated expressions of marginal or oppressed people, emphasizing their psychological rather than their sociopolitical functions.[1]

If there is a certain similarity and continuity detectable in Jamaican religious movements from Myalism in the eighteenth century through Revivalism in the nineteenth and Rastafarianism in the twentieth, it is not solely because they are lower class responses to colonial oppression. That explanation accounts only for the circumstances of the movements' development. Their shape and content are derived from an older, precolonial African tradition that posits a world in which, "under ideal circumstances, good prevails absolutely and exclusively." Such a perfect world is rarely achieved, however, because malevolent forces permeate the universe and produce evil through the malicious thoughts and feelings of selfish, antisocial people. Such people, placing personal goals above those of the community, employ ritual to satisfy their self-centered desires, that is, they practice magic or sorcery. To prevent the misfortune they occasion, and to maximize good fortune for the entire community are major functions of religious ritual which, unlike magic, is always community centered.

This is the religious tradition to which Afro-Jamaican religious movements belong. It is a dynamic, present-world-oriented tradition which refuses to

accept as natural dissension, poverty, corruption, illness, failure, oppression—
"all the negative, disappointing, tragic experiences of life. . . ." Believing these
evils to be caused by sorcery, this religious tradition claims to have the
weapons with which to eradicate them.[2] This tradition has been a powerful
catalyst for African and Afro-Jamaican resistance to European values and
control. It also explains why sociopolitical protest has usually been expressed in religious terms in Jamaica.[3]

Myalism, a religious movement which originated in eighteenth-century
Jamaica, is the first documented Jamaican religion cast in the "classical"
African mold, and an examination of Myalism can provide us with a model
for studying later Jamaican religious movements. Myal can be examined for
a hundred-year period from the 1760s to the 1860s at least. It emerged in the
1760s as a pan-African religious society to protect slaves against European
sorcery. By the early nineteenth century it had adopted Christian elements.
In 1831-32 Myalists assumed a leading role in the last Jamaican slave rebellion. The postslavery period saw it reemerge stronger than ever from a period
of persecution, acquiring new converts and openly challenging Christian missionaries in the early 1840s, only to be driven underground by the Jamaican
government. In the early 1860s it gained new life under the aegis of a religious revival whose missionary sponsorship Myalists soon rejected.

Although undoubtedly syncretic, Myalism demonstrates many of the
characteristics of classical Central African religious movements as outlined
recently by Willy de Craemer, Jan Vansina, and Renée C. Fox. First is a
collective group's acceptance of a new religious form consisting of rearranged
existing rituals, symbols, and beliefs combined occasionally with new beliefs.
Second, the originator is a charismatic leader, inspired by dreams or visions.
Third, the aim, in a culture which believes that good can and should prevail,
is to prevent misfortune and maximize good fortune for the community. As
a result Central African movements are always millennial and always involve
witch or sorcery hunting. Fourth, a movement must move beyond its original community. As it does, a specific group in each community assumes
responsibility for it, its members sometimes incorporating their own visions
in the movement, extending and modifying it in such a way that it may last
a quarter of a century or more despite unfulfilled millennial promises. A
movement may even seem to have disappeared when, in fact, political hos-
tility may have driven it underground to reemerge under more favorable
conditions. Fifth, the focus of all classical movements is a charm for the protection of the community from disease and death. Charms, however, may be
absent from or peripheral to movements which have adopted nonclassical
elements such as Christianity. Finally, de Craemer, Vansina, and Fox stress

that modern Central African movements have not been purely or even primarily reactions to the stresses of the colonial experience or modernization, but rather form "an integral part of the precolonial Central African tradition and they were primarily religious in nature."[4]

The planter-historian Edward Long was the first European to record the existence of the Myal religion, referring to it as a new society in the 1760s, open to *all*. Its initiation ritual, which he called the "myal dance," provided invulnerability to death caused by Europeans, that is, European sorcery. According to Long, candidates enacted a ritual of death and rebirth in the Myal dance by drinking a mixture of cold water and the herb-branched calalu* and then dancing until they reached a state of dissociation resembling death. The application of another mixture to the body revived the candidate.[5] While Long's is the only description of Myalism available for the eighteenth century, accounts of the 1830s and 1840s make it clear that Myalists believed that all misfortune—not just slavery—stemmed from malicious forces, embodied in the spirits of the dead. The Myal organization provided specialists—doctors—trained to identify the spirit causing the problem, exercise it, and prevent a recurrence. All problems, including bodily illness, were thought to stem from spiritual sources and required the performance of appropriate ritual.[6]

The appearance of the new Myal religion in the 1760s symbolized a spirit of cooperation among enslaved Africans of various ethnic backgrounds that had not hitherto been the case in Jamaica. Indeed, Myalism may actually have fostered pan-African cooperation where once only ethnic division had existed. The Africans who poured into Jamaica as slaves in the seventeenth and eighteenth centuries had entered a new, permanent situation in which *all* slaves regardless of previous rank or national origin, were considered equally inferior. All probably shared the common African conviction that malicious sorcery played a part in their misfortune.[7] Yet so strong was national identity, so linked was it to the rituals and customs that ensured survival, that despite their common predicament the different nations tended to isolate themselves from each other, none more so than the Akan. They organized exclusively Akan uprisings throughout most of the eighteenth century, led by ritual specialists who, like their counterparts in the Akan homeland, offered protection from European bullets. The Akan failed to recognize the inherent weakness of such national resistance in a heterogeneous slave population, but toward the end of the eighteenth century a trend towards pan-African solidarity may be detected. Several factors may have encouraged

*A member of the Solanaceae family, called West Indian spinach, and apparently narcotic when soaked, uncooked, in cold water.

this: the increase of Jamaica-born (Creole) slaves, who comprised 75 percent of the slave population by 1789; a decrease in Akan imports; a corresponding increase in Central African and Yoruba slaves; and Myalism which, by defining the cause of misfortune and its remedy, influenced the values and norms of plantation society for increasing numbers of slaves, and constituted an important form of social control by and for the enslaved.[8]

Part of the trend toward pan-African cooperation saw slave revolts organized along cooperative lines. Akan, Kongo, and Mandinka people participated in the slave revolt of 1798, and the rebellion of 1831-32 had a Creole stamp.[9] It was no coincidence that this uprising was popularly known as "The Baptist War," referring to the so-called "Native" or "Black" Baptists who led it and whose blend of African and European religious beliefs and practices was really Myalist, not Baptist.

Myalism had passed into a new stage after 1791 when it absorbed certain congenial aspects of the Baptist version of Christianity. During and after the American War of Independence, a number of United Empire Loyalists fled to the Bahamas, and some eventually made their way to Jamaica. Some of the Afro-American servants and slaves who accompanied them introduced the Baptist religion to Jamaica. Moses Baker, for example, aided by a Quaker planter, settled in St. James parish in 1791 to preach the Baptist faith to slaves. The geographical limits of Baker's following coincide almost exactly with the core area of an aggressive Myal movement of the 1840s. Because of strict laws against non-Church-of-England preachers, Baker had great difficulty maintaining regular contact with his followers; he could visit them only at night and could not hold Sunday services outside his employer's property. Nevertheless, he served congregations many miles apart.

The Black or Native Baptist preachers, as men like Baker came to be called, developed an organization that the English Baptists, Wesleyan Methodists and Presbyterians later found useful. They issued tickets indicating each individual's status—member, candidate, or inquirer—and for instruction they divided their flock into classes, each with its own leader. The leaders became almost totally independent of the preachers and ruled their classes with an iron hand. In time, Baker and his fellow preachers found it impossible to control the content of the leaders' teaching and their ritual, which grew less and less "orthodox" from the Baptist viewpoint.

Myalists extracted and emphasized two central elements of the Baptist faith because they seemed to correspond with beliefs or symbols already familiar to them—the inspiration of the Holy Spirit; and Baptism, in the manner of John the Baptist, by immersion. Some members actually referred to their church as "John the Baptist's Church." The leaders developed a technique for attaining possession by the Holy Spirit and "dreams" experienced in this state were crucial to a candidate's acceptance for baptism. Without them they could not be born again, "either by water or the Spirit." Today, descendants of nineteenth-century Central African immigrants in St. Thomas parish like to have their children baptized, even though they belong to the Kumina cult, because they believe that the sacrament confers on the child the Holy Spirit's special protection against evil spirits. They also profess a special attachment to Revivalists and Baptists who practice baptism by immersion in the river, the dwelling place of African spirits who are believed to protect them. The Afro-Jamaican religious tradition, then, has consistently reinterpreted Christianity in African, not European, cultural terms.

At the urging of Baker and his colleagues who were frustrated by this reinterpretation, the English Baptists sent a missionary to the north coast in 1814. His work among Baker's flock had scarcely begun when he died, and not until 1824 did his successor, Reverend Thomas Burchell, arrive. At Baker's urging most of his followers accepted Burchell's leadership, but many who joined the Baptist church eventually left, Baptist orthodoxy obviously had little to offer them, and they preferred a religion which combined Baptist and Myal elements in a way that deserves to be called Myalist rather than Black Baptist.[10]

The Myal notion of sin as sorcery, an offense not against God but against society, made it far more this-world oriented than the Baptist faith. Myal ritual offered a cure for society's ills which, since they were caused by sorcery, could be eradicated by antisorcery ritual. For this reason Myalism was far more relevant to many Afro-Jamaicans than any missionary version of the Christian faith. It attracted new followers on the north coast in the 1830s and 1840s and mounted anti-European offensives in both decades, demonstrating a continued Afro-Jamaican awareness of the major source of their misfortune in the nineteenth century.

Repression of a work-strike by slaves in St. James parish in late 1831 transformed the strike into a slave rebellion which spread to other parishes. The opportunity to eradicate European sorcery appeared to be at hand, and through the agency of a European prophet, the Reverend Thomas Burchell. In England at the time, Burchell was believed to be returning with the emancipation edict which the planters were thought to be withholding from the slaves. The year had been hard, with drought followed by floods, rumors concerning emancipation, and a fervent religious revival. No wonder the missionaries, articulate advocates of emancipation, appeared like prophets of the millennium.

The missionaries turned out not to be prophets after all, and instructed the slaves that, since Burchell could not bring freedom, they should return to work. The slaves, however, preferred to heed their leaders' message—that resistance was the work of God. Baptist and Presbyterian congregations accused their pastors of deserting them and of being "paid by the magistrates to deceive them" and threatened revenge. Severe repression of the rebellion followed, with deliberate military destruction of slave houses and kitchen gardens. Slave attendance at church declined, for the missionaries had been discredited by their failure to support the rebellion, by Burchell's failure to bring freedom, and, ironically, by the wave of persecution they faced from planters and Jamaican authorities who suspected them of having fomented the uprising.

Even though the rebellion did hasten the passage of the Emancipation Act in 1833, the coming of emancipation in 1834 did not confer the "full free" for which Afro-Jamaicans longed.[11] Four years of apprenticeship followed during which freed people had to continue working for their former owners, although wages were paid. For many, little had changed. The end of apprenticeship in 1838 brought the unwelcome news that the houses the slaves had built and the land they had cleared and cultivated on their masters' property were not theirs, and they were ordered to pay rent or move. Rent and wage disputes became the rule after 1838, hinging on the Afro-Jamaicans' determination that, if they had to work on the plantations, they would do so only for just wages and just rents. On their side planters were equally determined to get back in rent what they had paid in wages— to make free labor cheaper than slave, even as they mourned the loss of their slaves. Planters harassed adamant workers in a number of ways—workers' kitchen gardens and sometimes their homes were destroyed; garden produce was seized on its way to market and charges of theft brought against workers; eviction notices were issued. In many parts of the island there was an exodus from the plantations, both voluntary and involuntary, as former slaves sought work in the towns, or purchased marginal plantation land from financially ruined planters.[12]

By 1841 the wage situation had improved and rents had been lowered, but African immigrants were not introduced to provide competition in the labor market and drive wages down. A family of four or more could not subsist on plantation wages alone, or even on the food and income from a small plot of land; it needed both sources of income. Plantation laborers enjoyed the most comfort and security and had the best chance of saving money to purchase land if they worked on sugar estates with unused land in adjacent mountainous areas. These areas, such as the Plantain Garden River and Blue

Mountain Valley of St. Thomas-in-the-East and the enclosed basin of Upper Clarendon contained adjacent unused uplands usually well-watered by rivers and rainfall. Other districts were not so blessed, notably the lowland coastal areas of St. James, Trelawny and the plains of Westmoreland. Here all tillable lowland was planted with sugar cane, and workers' provision grounds had to be located in hills and mountains a considerable distance from the plantations. These plantation workers, therefore, had to divide their time unproductively between their lowland jobs and their mountain plots, wasting many hours traveling between the two. Capricious rainfall and poor soil made food crop cultivation unremunerative but affected sugar cultivation less, so sugar estates in this area continued to prosper while those elsewhere failed, and proprietors here did not feel the need to break up their adjacent hill and mountain lands for sale to workers who, more than most, remained trapped on the estates. The results were still evident in the twentieth century with poor, unsubstantial houses reflecting the fact that people had neither time nor motivation to improve their estate dwellings, nor to erect more than lean-tos in the mountains.[13]

The hardships experienced in the northern Jamaican parishes of St. James and Trelawny, center of Myalism in the 1820s, 1830s, and early 1840s, produced a revival among Myalists which gained the movement new members as it set out to eradicate the sorcery that was causing misfortune. This new stage of the Myal movement began in December 1841 and lasted until repression drove it underground in November of the following year. A plantation movement for the reasons described above, it began on Spring estate on the St. James coast about six miles from Montego Bay, and eventually affected some twenty-two plantation villages.

Since 1838 a number of unexpected deaths had occurred in the Spring estate village; these were ascribed to obeah, which was then blamed for every misfortune. During Christmas of 1841, tenants of Spring invited Myalists from nearby Ironshore estate to cleanse Spring of obeah, and everyone but the Presbyterians in the village participated in the ceremonies. A second Myal band from Flower Hill estate performed the antiobeah ritual on Blue Hole estate in July or August 1842. Villagers from Millennium Hall and Palmyra estates requested Myal help in September. The ritual performances increased and spread southwest and southeast of Spring, encompassing sixteen or seventeen sugar estate villages in St. James, bounded on the south by the Montego River. By October 1842 the movement had crossed parish boundaries, entering Trelawny and, some said, Westmoreland. Although primarily a north coast phenomenon, it turned up as far away as St. Thomas-in-the-Vale the same year.[14]

The Myal religion in the 1840s recognized three grades of membership—Archangels, Angels, and Ministering Angelics. The Archangels, both men and women, were the leaders whose chief function was that of divination, which the other two ranks represented lower levels of expertise and had special ritual functions. The Angels spoke readily of their visions and their ability to detect obeah and its devotees. The Ministering Angelics usually operated in groups of nine to twenty people and concentrated on making converts, digging up buried obeah charms and catching shadows. Myal believers were of both sexes, single as well as married, and of all ages, although some observers commented on the large number of young men among them. They led well-regulated lives and did not drink alcohol. When engaged in anti-obeah activities they wore cords or handkerchiefs tied tightly around their heads and waists and carried bottles of liquid and other ritual objects.[15]

Myalists in 1841-42 preached in prophetic and millennial terms that they were God's angels, appointed by Him to do His work. God, they said, had observed that the world had become "contrary" and so "he appointed we for to put it right again. . . ." Myalists were called "to do the work of the Lord, and do it, they must. . . . Their bodies may be punished here, but above all they will be rewarded according to their zeal. . . ." When urged to return to the plantation labor they had deserted, Myalists retorted, "we cannot keep peace till Jesus tell us to keep it. The spirit is all over the world." Aware that their message would fall on more or less orthodox Christian ears—indeed, intending it to do so—Myalists explained that although their teachings were not in the Bible, "God ordain it for all that." And they justified their mission by claiming a new dispensation—"Minister to baptize them right, theirs is the true Baptism, and foretime God speak to his prophets and disciples, and why not now also?" The Myal task, they preached, was to clear the land for Jesus Christ, who was coming among them, and they predicted that their movement would soon spread throughout Jamaica.[16]

Clearing the land for Jesus Christ meant eradicating obeah through special public rituals which only Myalists could perform. The first, a ceremony to discover the sources of obeah, required the drinking of a mixture containing the root of a lily plant. This, followed by singing and dancing, produced a state of dissociation in which participants claimed guidance by the Myal spirit to buried obeah charms and, in some cases, to the person responsible for burying them. The offending objects would then be dug up, and if a guilty person was uncovered, he or she would be subjected to a trial and ordeal, thereby forcing a confession and a vow of repentance. The Myal dance, usually held in the evening, started as early as six o'clock and often did not end until one in the morning. Since it could take more than a single performance to achieve results, the dance could continue for many nights.[17]

Most accounts of Myal antiobeah activity fail to provide detailed information about either the persons involved or the diagnoses of Myal doctors. On occasion, old Africans were accused of practicing obeah, and if many Myalists were young men, self-promotion might well have been a cause of their accusing the elderly of sorcery. Such accusations might also reflect a Creole-African cleavage owing to fear of African ritual powers or simply a fear of job competition from new African arrivals. On at least one occasion African recaptives rescued from a Cuban slave ship and settled in St. James were accused of obeah. On Running Gut estate in St. James such accusations led to a riot. Millennium Hall Myalists accused a colored shopkeeper of obeah because he testified against them in court. They probably already had grievances against him—both his color and his occupation symbolized privilege, and plantation workers all over Jamaica resented their dependence on estate shops. Competition for choice estate jobs also caused conflict, and on one occasion a Myal doctor diagnosed that an estate head stillerman who lost his job had been bewitched by his successor who had stolen his shadow.[18]

Myal wrath targeted two groups of Europeans—planters and missionaries. "I cannot do other work but my Lord work," Myalists tried for disturbing the peace said constantly (Myalism was not at this time illegal). Since "other work" meant plantation labor, the work stoppages connected with Myalism in 1841-42 may well have been a form of "industrial action" against employers. The planters, at any rate, reacted as if this were indeed the case, summoned the police to stop performances of Myal ritual on their estates. Police action produced considerable unrest—people attacked constables on their way to make arrests, threatened to burn down a police station, and denounced the authorities, beginning with the Queen and proceeding downward to the governor and local magistrates.[19]

The missionaries were as alarmed as the planters, and denounced the new Myal prophecies. Myalists reacted to missionary castigation and interference abusively and aggressively. When Reverend Hope M. Waddell, a Presbyterian with many parishioners on the affected estates, tried to break up the Myal ritual on Blue Hole by accusing female Myalists of madness, members turned on him in anger:

"They are not mad." "They have the spirit."
"You must be mad yourself, and had best go away." "Let the women go on, we don't want you." 'Who brought you here?" "What do you want with us?"

Most estates had meeting houses erected by missionary organizations, and Myalists attempted to gain possession of these as well as missionary churches.

In one case a Baptist class voluntarily turned over their meeting house to Myalists. Thus, competition for members became an issue between European missionaries and Myalists.[20]

Myalism made an attempt at that time to create the more perfect world the missionaries themselves had promised but had failed to deliver—a state where spiritual salvation matched economic and social self-sufficiency. The missionaries might buy land and create new settlements, they might champion Afro-Jamaicans in petition after petition, but they were not part of the island's power structure, although when the chips were down they tended to support it. They had neither economic nor political power. They could lighten but not eradicate the burdens of the people. In 1841—fifty years after the Baptist word was first preached on the north coast—Myalists offered something more hopeful: quite simply, the millennium.[21]

Severe measures taken by the authorities against Myalists temporarily checked its public manifestations. Within three years, however, the dance was performed again on Trelawny estates, and sporadic accounts of Myal practice continued to trickle in from various parishes throghout the troubled 1850s.[22]

Through their continued control of an economy based on monoculture as well as their control of the government, Jamaican planters perpetuated the very afflictions Myalism had been designed to counteract. They understood correctly that Myalism threatened that control. Had they let Myalism as a public regeneration movement go unchecked in 1842 it may well have challenged European control more aggressively as it had done in 1831-32.

The late 1840s and the 1850s were years of extreme hardship for Jamaicans. Severe cholera, smallpox, and measles epidemics struck in the 1850s. Drought and food shortages marked both decades, and manmade hardships like lower wages, higher prices and taxes combined with disease to create an atmosphere of despair and apocalypse. These festering troubles produced periodic eruptions. Violent protests occurred in 1859 over extortionist road tolls in Westmoreland and a land tenure dispute in Trelawny.[23] An occasional educated urban Jamaican warned of bloody revolution, but after the riots of 1859, working-class Jamaicans resorted, not to greater violence, but to restorative ritual just as they had done in 1840.

Beginning in the Moravian church and spreading rapidly to Baptist and Wesleyan congregations, a movement known as the Great Revival swept over Jamaica; it subsided in 1861 but resurfaced in 1866 in the wake of the Morant Bay tragedy of late 1865. The revival soon left missionaries behind, frowning in disapproval at the Myal elements such as dancing, drumming, and spirit possession which revivalists practiced—evidence that Myalism, far from defunct, had been kept alive by the struggle against misfortune and evil through the forties and fifties. It could be argued that the Great Revival was more Myalist than Christian. Certainly when Myalism once more tested its strength against Christianity, Myalism proved the more vital of the two. In subsequent years black revivalist sects multiplied and flourished. The Myal movement was once more undergoing transformation.[24] "Eventually," according to de Craemer, Vansina and Fox, "all movements end up being replaced by others that seem very similar to outsiders, but look brand new to the congregations." The acid test comes when people feel that misfortune is not being eradicated, and they turn to what they hope will prove to be a more effective movement, receiving at least "a sense of renewal" from it. The new movement must show many of the features of the old, however, and "This the underlying process which accounts for the fact that all Central African religious movements are variants of a single tradition. However different they may be, they retain the attributes of the paradigm."[25]

The visions revealed in the wake of the Great Revival may not all have been as revolutionary as the following warning from "A Son of Africa" posted on a wharf gate in Lucea, Hanover in 1865, but it is nevertheless suggestive of the Great Revival's conception of the nature of misfortune at that time:

> I heard a Voice speaking to me in the year 1864, saying, "Tell the Sons and Daughters of Africa, that a great deliverance will take place for them from the hand of Oppression; for, said the Voice, they are oppressed by Government, by Magistrates, by Proprietors, and by Merchants." And this voice also said "tell them to call a solemn Assembly, and to sanctify themselves for the day of deliverance which will surely take place; but, if the People will not hearken, I will bring the Sword into the land to chastise them for their disobedience, and for the iniquities which they have committed. And the Sword will come from America. If the people depend upon their Arms, and upon our Queen, and forget Him who is our God, they will be greatly mistaken, and the mistakes will lead to great distress". . . . But great will be the deliverance of the sons and daughters of Africa, the children of Nlaweh . . . for the Voice said, if we wait until the thing takes place before we cry unto Him, the cry will be in vain, but if we pray truly from our hearts, and humble ourselves we have no need to fear. If not . . . there will be Gog and Magog to battle.[26]

Even after the bloody suppression of the Morant Bay disturbances of 1865 in which the original demonstration had been led by a separatist preacher, Revivalists were not cowed, nor did they go underground as they might have. Sharing a common core of belief and a spirit of solidarity similar to

76   MONICA SCHULER

that of the Myalists, they defied official attempts to intimidate them. Threatened in 1866 with official action if he did not curb his noisy Revival meetings, a Westmoreland leader responded that "he would bring a thousand people from Hanover and he would see who could hinder him." The official fumed: "These people are under the impression that they can do what they like in their own place. . . ." He was right. They did.[27]

The Myal tradition formed the core of a strong and self-confident counterculture. It guaranteed that none of the evils of the postslavery period would be accepted passively, but would be fought ritually and publicly. This would lead inevitably to periodic confrontations with island authorities or any group considered to be the perpetrators of misfortune, destroyers of harmony, the most dangerous sorcerers of a particular time.[28]

NOTES

Written with the support of a grant from the Wenner-Gren Foundation for Anthropological Research.

1. See, for example, George Eaton Simpson, "Religions of the Caribbean," and Raymond T. Smith, "Religion in the Formation of West Indian Society: Guyana and Jamaica," in *The African Diaspora: Interpretive Essays*, Martin L. Kilson and Robert I. Rotberg (Cambridge, 1976), pp. 280-11, 312-41.

2. For a study of such movements see Willy de Craemer, Jan Vansina, and Renée C. Fox, "Religious Movements in Central Africa: A Theoretical Study," *Comparative Studies in Society and History* 18, no. 4 (October 1976): 458-75; for the attributes of such movements and their goals see especially pp. 460-61, 467-68. I am grateful to Professor Jan Vansina for bringing this article to my attention.

3. Leonard E. Barrett, *The Rastafarians: A Study in Messianic Cultism in Jamaica*, Caribbean Monograph Series no. 6. (Rio Pedras, 1968), pp. 193-94. Barrett cites Madeline Kerr, *Personality and Conflict in Jamaica* (Liverpool, 1963), on the subject of the religious nature of Jamaican poltical movements.

4. It is possible that the word *myal* is of Central African origin. Descendants of Central African immigrants in St. Thomas parish, members of the Kumina cult, describe powerful possession by ancestral spirits as "catching myal." Since from the start the Myal religion seems to have been associated with no one African group, it was probably a blend of West and Central African beliefs that arose out of the needs and traditions of plantation slaves of diverse ethnic origins. Although de Craemer et al. have limited their analysis to Central Africa, the area they know best, their findings may be at least partially applicable to West Africa. See de Craemer et al., "Religious Movements," pp. 465-74.

5. Edward Long, *The History of Jamaica*, 3 vols. (London, 1970), 2: 416-17; Orlando Patterson, *The Sociology of Slavery: An Analysis of the Origins, Developement, and Structure of Negro Slave Society in Jamaica*. (London, 1967; Rutherford, N.J., 1969), pp. 186-87.

6. Many Myal doctors worked in plantation hospitals during slavery. Reverend Hope Masterton Waddell, *Twenty-Nine Years in the West Indies and Central Africa* (London,

1970) pp. 137-38; James M. Philippo, *Jamaica, Its Past and Present State* (London, 1969), pp. 248-49; T. W. Jackson to Robert Bruce, 4 November 1842, enclosed in no. 64, Earl of Elgin to Lord Stanley, 28 December 1842, CO 137/264.

7. In Jamaica, sorcery is known as *obeah*. All African societies have belived that sorcery is essentially antisocial, have tended to attribute most forms of misfortune to it and, consequently, fear sorcerers. See Mary Douglas, *Purity and Danger* (New York, 1966), pp. 107-8; John S. Mbiti, *African Religion and Philosophy* (New York, 1970), pp. 261-63.

8. Patterson, *Sociology of Slavery*, pp. 141-46, 153-54; Monica Schuler, "Akan Slave Rebellions in the British Caribbean," *Savacou* I, no. 1 (June 1970): 8-31; Philip D. Curtin, *The Atlantic Slave Trade: A Census* (Madison, Wis., 1969), p. 160. There is now a growing realization that religions like Myalism constituted vital selfgoverning communities. See, for instance, Edward Kamau Brathwaite, "Caliban, Ariel, and Unprospero in the Conflict of Creolization: A Study of the Slave Revolt in Jamaica in 1831-32," in *Comparative Perspectives on Slavery in New World Plantation Societies*, ed. Vera Rubin and Arthur Tuden (New York, 1977), p. 57.

9. For 1798 rebellion see *Journals of the House of Assembly of Jamaica*, 1797-1802, pp. 106-14.

10. For the history of Black Baptists in Jamaica see W. J. Gardner, *A History of Jamaica* (London, 1971), pp. 343-53, 357-60; Waddell, *Twenty-Nine Years*, pp. 25-27, 35-36; Philip D. Curtin, *Two Jamaicas: The Role of Ideas in a Tropical Colony, 1830-1865* (New York, 1970), pp. 32-33; Beverly Brown, "George Liele: Black Baptist and Pan-Africanist, 1750-1826," *Savacou* vols. 11/12 (September 1975): 58-67. The practice of demanding visions as signs of conversion was still common among Jamaica Revivalists in the early twentieth century; see Martha Beckwith, *Black Roadways: A Study Jamaican Folk Life* (Chapel Hill, 1929), pp. 163, 165, 166-67. This practice appears to be a feature of African diaspora religion; see, for instance, Melville J. Herskovits and Frances Herskovits, *Trinidad Village* (New York, 1964), pp. 199-202; George P. Rawick, ed., *God Struck Me Dead*, 19 vols., vol. 19, *The American Slave: A Composite Biography* (Westport, 1972); Joseph G. Moore, "Religion of Jamaica Negroes: A Study of Afro-Jamaican Acculturation," (Ph. D. diss., Evanston, Ill., 1953), p. 150. In the 1920s Beckwith noted the continued symbolism of water among Revivalists. See also her transcription of a Revivalist hymn dating back to the 1840s "River Jordan," Beckwith, *Black Roadways*, pp. 167-68, 175, 181.

11. Mary Reckord, "The Slave Rebellion of 1831," *Jamaica Journal* 3 (June 1969): 25-31; Curtin, *Two Jamaicas*, pp. 85-88; Waddell, *Twenty-Nine Years*, pp. 50, 52, 55-56, 63, 74. Barry Higman has noted the essentially rural nature of the 1831-32 rebellion, stressing that it occurred in "monocultural sugar areas where the system of colour and status was most highly developed, and where the heavy rate of natural decrease was placing stresson the system." See Barry W. Higman, *Slave Population and Economy in Jamaica, 1807-1834* (Cambridge, 1976), p. 230. For slave mortality between 1817 and 1832 see pp. 105-6. The context of the 1841-42 Myal movement was essentially the same. For a rebellion in Demerara see Schuler, "Akan Slave Rebellions," pp. 24-27.

12. Douglas Hall, *Free Jamaica, 1838-1865: An Economic History* (London and Edinburgh, 1969), pp. 8, 10, 20-21, 117-18, 158, 168-69, 171, 172, 182-83, 193, 235. Sir Lionel Smith to Lord Glenelg, no. 8, 5 January 1839, and enclosed Stipendiary Magistrates' reports, CO 137/241; idem, no. 74, 6 April 1839, and enclosed Stipendiary Magistrates' reports, CO 137/242; idem, no. 53, 25 February 1839, and enclosed Stipendiary Magistrates' reports, CO 137/242. Hugh Paget, "The Free Village System in Jamaica," in *Apprenticeship and Emancipation* (Mona, Jamaica) pp. 45-48. State of Agriculture, *Votes of the House of Assembly of Jamaica* (VHAJ), October-December 1845, Appendix no. 66, p. 713.

13. Monica Schuler, " 'Yerri, Yerri, Koongo': A Social History of Liberated African Immigration into Jamaica, 1841-1867" (Ph.D. diss., University of Wisconsin, 1977). Lord Olivier, *Jamaica: The Blessed Isle* (London, 1936), pp. 135-37, 197.

14. The reference to deaths on Spring estates suggests that the high mortality noted by Higman on the last years of slavery was still a significant factor as the decade of the 1840s opened. Higman, *Slave Population*, pp. 105-16. Walter Finlayson Report, 31 December 1838, enclosed in no. 11, Sir Lionel Smith to Lord Glenelg, 5 January 1839, CO 137/241. *Jamaica Standard and Royal Gazette*, n.s., 64, 308, 30 September 1842, 1:2-4; 320, 14 October 1842, 1:2-3; 322, 17 October 1842, 1:4; 326, 21 October 1842, 2:3; 334, 31 October 1842, 2:3-4; 341, 8 November 1842, 3:1-2; 350, 18 November 1842, 2:2-3. Waddell, *Twenty-Nine Years*, pp. 53, 137, 191-94; J. H. Buchner, *The Moravians in Jamaica, History of the Mission of the United Brethren's Church to the Negroes in the Island of Jamaica, From the Year 1754 to 1854* (London, 1854), p. 139.

15. The concept of a dual soul is central to Myal beliefs. See William Bascom, *The Yoruba of Southwestern Nigeria* (New York, 1969), p. 71; Moore, "Religion of Jamaica," pp. 33-34, 152; George Eaton Simpson, "The Shango Cult in Nigeria and Trinidad," *American Anthropologist* 64, no. 6 (December 1962): 1213; Geoffrey Parrinder, *West African Religion: A Study of Beliefs and Practices of the Akan, Ewe, Yoruba, Ibo, and Kindred People* (London, 1961), pp. 113-14; Karl Laman, *The Kongo*, 3 vols. (Lund, 1962), 3: 75, 95-98, for African beliefs in a dual soul. See also *Jamaica Standard*, n.s., 64, 320, 14 October 1842, 1:1; 308, 30 September 1842, 1:2; Buchner, *Moravians*, 139; Waddell, *Twenty-Nine Years*, quoting from *Cornwall Chronicle*, pp. 192-93.

16. Waddell, *Twenty-Nine Years*, p. 188; *Jamaica Standard*, n.s., 64, 308, 30 September 1842, 1:3-4; 320, 14 October 1842, 1:1; 334, 31 October 1842, 2:3.

17. *Jamaica Standard*, n.s., 64, 320, 14 October 1842, 1:3; 350, 18 November 1842, 2:2-3; Buchner, *Moravians*, p. 139; Waddell, *Twenty-Nine Years*, pp. 193-94. Drums and rattles were not mentioned in any of the eyewitness accounts of the 1841-42 Myal ceremonies, but Beckwith observed the use of both in the 1920s. Beckwith, *Black Roadways*, pp. 148-49.

18. Sir Charles Metcalfe to Lord John Russell, no. 80, 18 May 1840, CO 137/249; Daniel Kelly to Robert Bruce, 14 June 1843, enclosed in no. 140; Earl of Elgin to Lord Stanley, 29 July 1843, CO 137/274; Waddell, *Twenty-Nine Years*, pp. 188, 193-94; *Jamaica Standard*, n.s., 64, 308, 30 September 1842, 1:3; 350, 18 November 1842, 2:2-3; Hall, *Free Jamaica*, pp. 208-9. Higman's analysis of the stresses that resulted from increased competition for skilled plantation jobs after 1820 and that contributed to the 1831 rebellion is relevant here. See Higman, *Slave Population*, pp. 231-32. The Myal specialist who diagnosed the problem of the head stillerman in 1842 used a stone called an "amber" in the divination process. This was still used by Myalists in the early twentieth century. See Beckwith, *Black Roadways*, pp. 154, 159.

19. *Jamaica Standard*, n.s., 64, 308, 30 September 1842, 1:2-4; 326, 21 October 1842, 1:3-4.

20. Waddell, *Twenty-Nine Years*, pp. 190-92; *Jamaica Standard*, n.s., 64, 308, 30 September 1842, 1:2; Buchner, *Moravians*, pp. 140-41.

21. Curtin, *Two Jamaicas*, pp. 92-93, 159-60, 162-69; Inez Knibb Sibley, *The Baptists of Jamaica, 1793-1965* (Kingston, 1965), pp. 30-31.

22. Magistrate Lawson to Robert Bruce, 1 May 1843, enclosed in no. 140, Earl of Elgin to Lord Stanley, 29 July 1843, CO 137/274; *Falmouth Post*, vol. 12, 34, 25 August 1846, 2:1; Bourke Grievance, December 1859, VHAJ November-December 1859, Appendix no. 4, pp. 224-25; Alexander Fyfe to Hugh Austin, 24 January 1854, enclosed in no. 4, Sir Henry Barkly to Duke of Newcastle, 21 February 1854, CO 137/322; J. A. Dillon to W. G. Stewart, 14 August 1856, enclosed in no. 58, E. W.

Bell to Henry Labouchere, 25 November 1856, CO 137/332. See also Curtin, *Two Jamaicas*, p. 170.

23. Hall, *Free Jamaica*, pp. 88-97; Curtin, *Two Jamaicas*, pp. 151-52. William Bell to Hugh Austin, 17 July 1854, enclosed in no. 101, Major Berkeley to Earl Grey, 18 September 1854, CO 137/324. For Toll Gate Riots see Charles Darling to Edward Bulwer-Lytton, no. 48, 25 March 1859, CO 137/344 and enclosures. For Trelawny disturbances see Darling to Duke of Newcastle, no. 103, 9 August 1859, and idem, no. 114, 5 September 1859, CO 137/346.

24. For the Great Revival see Curtin, *Two Jamaicas*, pp. 168-71. Martha Beckwith recognized the Myal ancestry of nineteenth- and twentieth-century Revivalism in Jamaica. See Beckwith, *Black Roadways*, p. 59, especially, but also pp. 142-82 for discussion of Myal and Revival sects and practices.

25. de Craemer et al., "Religious Movements," p. 467.

26. "Intelligence from Lucea," in *Falmouth Post*, 31, no. 47 (16 June 1865): 2. The reference to a sword coming out of America may have been a result of the impact of the Civil War and rumors of the expansion of United States slavery into the Caribbean.

27. E. Alcock to H. A. Whitelocke, 17 December 1866, enclosed in no. 32, Sir John Grant to Earl of Carnarvon, 23 February 1867, CO 137/422. Reverend Anthony Davidson, Rector of Hanover, claimed that around Arpil-May 1865 he had noticed a dramatic reduction in church attendance from about 2,000 to 1,400, and that at the time of the Morant Bay disturbance in October, attendance had dwindled to "exceeding few" and had not increased since the end of the disturbances. He credited the decrease to the people's attending their own revival meetings. See Reverend Anthony Davidson evidence, Jamaica Royal Commission, 1866, Part II, P. P. 1866, XXX (3683-I), 638:1-2.

28. For two twentieth-century manifestations of this type of confrontation see the prophet Bedward's announcement in 1920 that he would ascend into heaven, the whites would be destroyed, and the reign of Bedwardism (the Jamaica Baptist Free Church was his creation) would commence on earth, Beckwith, *Black Roadways*, pp. 168-71; and the various teachings and manifestations of Rastafarianism. Barrett, *The Rastafarians*. Rastafarian leaders are politically astute, and have a sophisticated understanding of the causes of contemporary Jamaican problems, as Barrett demonstrates. The time is now ripe for a reconsideration of such movements in the light of African religious tradition.

5

JAMAICAN JONKONNU
AND RELATED CARIBBEAN FESTIVALS

Judith Bettelheim

The Jonkonnu, or John Canoe, has a very long tradition as a folk festival in Jamaica. Documentary evidence suggests that at least since the beginning of the eighteenth century, masked and costumed performers have paraded the streets at Christmas. Indeed, Jonkonnu remains a very popular national festival in contemporary Jamaica, and might be regarded as a pan-Caribbean festival with a long and complicated history. From Belize in the southwest to Bermuda and North Carolina in the north, variations of this type of Jamaican folk festival are integrated with other Christmas festivities.

This chapter has two goals. The first is to try to establish the artistic geography of Jamaican Jonkonnu, the peculiar context in which it developed, and its contributory streams of European and African characteristics. The second goal is to determine the Jamaican artistic relationship to the other Christmas festivals in Bermuda, Nassau, St. Kitts, Nevis, and Belize. It is expected that an analysis of the heritage of these festivals may not only clarify their historical components, but also explain their transformation through time.

The most elaborate eighteenth-century description of the Jamaican festivals may be found in the narrative of Edward Long, an English planter politician and author of the *History of Jamaica*, published in 1774. Long's history documents elaborate street performances which he undoubtedly observed first hand during his long residence in the island during the 1750s and 1760s. These street performances included both masked characters performing in mime as well as troupes of players acting out scenes from English theatrical plays. Other chroniclers of the time also refer to black dancers wearing strange face masks and horned headdresses. The descriptions, especially the emphasis by Long, strongly suggest two separate groups performing independently and representing two different traditions of art and theater. One of these traditions was distinctly African, and the other was derived from English folk theater.

Edward Long's account is of special interest, and deserves a careful reading. Long not only describes the performers, especially the cow tails, cow horns, swords, but he also notes that the principal dancer wore a visor-type mask with a mouth section supported by boar tusks, and gave the name John Connú to this central character. Long continues to explain that both the parade and the main dancer are an honorable memorial to John Conny, an active, successful black merchant near Axim along the Guinea Coast around 1720. As far as can be ascertained, this is the first time that a specific name and geographical identification are given to the street festival. Later writers copied Long's account, varying the spelling. British-influenced writers spell the name John Canoe, while in contemporary Jamaica the spelling more closely reflects the pronunciation. The phonetic transformation of the name John Conny to Jonkonnu is still the source of academic dispute, although at least since the later eighteenth century the Christmas parade has been known as Jonkonnu.

This much can be ascertained: John Conny was an important historical person. He worked for the Brandenburg Company, and was about fifty years old in 1721. Conny ruled over three Brandenburg trading forts, Pokoso, Takrama, and Akoda on the coast of Ghana. By 1724, his influence had been in decline, and when the Dutch took over the Great Fredricksburg Castle, Conny moved inland and took up residence at the court of Opoku Ware, the king of Ashante.[1] Undoubtedly the reputation of this African arrived via the Gold Coast slaves sold throughout the Caribbean. Why the name should have particular prominence in Jamaica, however, is uncertain and there are many other theories concerning the origin of the name Jonkonnu.[2] It is perhaps safe to conclude tentatively that a combination of linguistic and political factors produced the nomenclature prevailing since the eighteenth century.

Today the name Jonkonnu in Jamaica connotes an exclusively male entourage of costumed dancers as well as the principal character. They perform not only at Christmas, but on important state occasions. The Jonkonnu performance is secular, and the correspondent with Christmas is merely historical. Originally, Christmas was one of the few periods when the slaves were relieved of their duties. This formed an appropriate season for festivities as all normal business activity on the island was halted by official decree and all males were called up for military service, thereby augmenting the population in the larger towns. To the present the urban populations have formed the principal spectators at Jonkonnu parades.

One persistent myth is that Jonkonnu is no longer celebrated, that it is an old-fashioned tradition which died with slavery, and is strongly deprecated by most Jamaicans, especially the anglophile middle classes. While the attitude toward the festivals reveals some ambivalence on the part of some Jamaicans, it is nevertheless certain that in some sectors of the population, and in some areas, participation is highly valued, and the spectacle itself has broad support. Curiously enough, eyewitness accounts of Jonkonnu festivals in Jamaica during the nineteenth and early twentieth centuries are virtually nonexistent. One possible explanation for this absence may be that historians and travelers reported on urban festivities, and the urban pressures against folk traditions forced the Jonkonnu "underground." Yet the tradition persisted in the rural areas. Recent interviews with performers in St. Thomas, Kingston, and Savanna-la-Mar tend to support the assumption that the festivals never ceased entirely among the rural folk, and the oldest performers recall troupes dating back to the 1920s.

The modern resurrection dates back to 1951-52 when the *Daily Gleaner*, the largest newspaper in the island, sponsored a national "John Canoe" competition. This competition attracted more than fifty bands across the island, and an audience of more than 20,000 viewed the final competition. It is perhaps reasonable to assume that the bands and their popularity did not suddenly materialize, but rather evoked the memories and the nostalgia of a large latent group of potential performers and spectators.

The history of the Jonkonnu parade indicates either an isolated festivity associated with a specific Great House, or plantation on the island, or a general island-wide activity in which slave and free non-Europeans participated. Nevertheless, the ensemble of costumed dancers differs considerably throughout the island. And these regional differences are found in the characters, the costumes, and the performance styles.

Traditional Jonkonnu most often includes as core participants the cowhead, the horsehead, the devil, different categories of warriors and Indians, as well as a character called Pitchy Patchy. The English-influenced troupes, however, never include animal characters. Instead, their core members are usually a king and queen, courtiers, and incidental characters based on the English masquerade, such as a sweeper, a jockey, and a sailor. These two types of troupes dress differently—the English-influenced troupes wearing "fancy dress" period costumes. The character of Actor Boy appears in a few historical accounts. It is highly probable that Actor Boy was originally derived from "speaking groups," rather than the Jonkonnu who always perform in mime. There are about ten other characters which can be added to either type of ensemble at will. Jonkonnu music is essentially "fife and drum" music. The band can consist of a bamboo fife, a bass and rattling drum, a banjo, and a grater; but the required minimum are fife and drums.

Traditionally the planter class sponsored both Masquerade actor groups and Jonkonnu groups. The strongest British influence is discernible in the Masquerade groups, which come in large part from the western Jamaican parishes of St. Elizabeth, Westmoreland, and Hanover. Although all Jamaican troupes are generically known as Jonkonnu, the troupes from these parishes insist that prior to the 1951 and 1952 competitions, they called themselves masquerades. One of the numerous results of the "official" publicity from these competitions is that all Christmas festival troupes are now known as Jonkonnu. It is also the generic name employed by government agencies, such as the Festival Commission or the Jamaica School of Dance.

In attempting to sort out the possible sources of traditional Jonkonnu characters, one can look to either Africa or England. The animal characters of horsehead and cowhead appear to be the most direct legacies of an African heritage. Historically, another legacy may exist in the form of a house or ship headdress, but this question will be considered later and in any event, this headdress is no longer extant. Recent field work in Jamaica confirms the above hypothesis.

In a personal interview in July 1976, Mr. Theodore Sealy, the top organizer of the 1951 and 1952 competitions, recalled his impressions of some of the more spectacular troupes. In his view, the most elegant troupes danced with "grace and favor," and his descriptions implied that despite the stylization and polish of the folk bands, the dichotomous underlying influences of Africa and Europe were still readily apparent. The competitions highlighted two different styles. Some included kings, queens, bishops, and courtiers—representations of an early modern Europe. Some troupes performed European dances. Other troupes, however, demonstrated a strong African influence. Their performance style and the importance of animal characters recalled a powerful African aesthetic.

Another judge during the competitions, the celebrated comedian, Ranny Williams, concurred with this opinion. He explained that the distinctiveness of the groups from the St. Ann's Bay area came from the outstanding dance performances and frightful visages of cowhead and horsehead. The fascinating aspect of this comes from the fact that the St. Ann's Bay troupes all came from mountain villages, with established traditions of free communities and where the African roots were probably more profound.

Agreeing with the distinctions made by Ranny Williams and Theodore Sealy, Mr. Cooper, who played "Actor Boy" in the British-influenced Westmoreland Troupe, answered my question: "Have you ever seen the cowhead and the horsehead?" with the reply: "I've seen it. . .but we don't play those games." For to the contemporary Jamaican, the horsehead and cowhead are African symbols, powerful, wild, and scary.

Although we cannot be certain of the forms these headdresses took in the past, eighteenth- and nineteenth-century reports do mention the wearing of cowhorns, with or without the associated face mask, more often than they mention the horsehead. The current Jonkonnu cowhead attire is made from a pan, or from half a shell of the coconut, with holes allowing for the insertion of real horns. This headdress is worn over a headwrap and a wire screen mask with painted facial features, common to all Jonkonnu performers. The horsehead is made from a mule's skull, equipped with an articulated jaw, and attached to a pole. It is painted, eyes are added, and the player covers himself with a piece of cloth. In traditional Jonkonnu, the rest of the costume is usually left up to the individual performer. It most often takes the form of white tennis shoes, pants, and a shirt in contrasting colors and patterns.

Though the cowhead is pretty ubiquitous, the horsehead only appears in certain Jonkonnu troupes. The two horseheads that I interviewed learned their craft while living in rural villages. One, Jim Robinson, from Beeston Springs, Westmoreland, said that before joining a Jonkonnu troup he always used to act alone. In fact, playing horsehead at political rallies, in front of stores, and during the Christmas season used to be Robinson's major source of income. In 1951 he won first prize in the national Jonkonnu competitions.

Another character that may reflect an African heritage (as well as a British one) is Pitchy Patchy. He is usually the most flamboyant and athletic troupe member and appears in both Jonkonnu and Masquerade groups. Pitchy Patchy's costume is made of layered strips of brightly colored fabric. Contemporary oral tradition claims that this costume is based on a vegetal prototype. In fact, vegetal costumes are associated with historical Jonkonnu. I. M. Belisario's 1837 sketches of a Kingston Christmas festival include a Jack-in-the-Green character who is completely covered with coconut leaves (palm fronds). This Jack-in-the-Green was named after a similarly costumed individual who followed the chimney sweeps around London during May Day celebrations. The London figure wore evergreen boughs. The substitution of palm fronds echoes a strong West African masquerade tradition.[3] What I am suggesting is that the cloth Pitchy Patchy costume may once have been a vegetal one. The transition from a costume of layered straw or palm fronds to one of layered cloth or paper strips is quite plausible, as it would reflect the increased distribution of such materials, an increase in prosperity, or merely a visual statement of an urban image rather than a rural one.

A brief discussion of the masquerade troupe from Savanna-la-Mar, Westmoreland, will elucidate the manner in which British Masquerade has influenced the Jamaican practice. The group I am about to discuss entered the 1951 and 1952 competitions as a Jonkonnu troupe and won first prize as the best all island Jonkonnu troupe. When I saw them perform on Christmas Day 1976, there were only six players . . . Captain, Flower Girl, Sailor Boy, Babu, and two Pitchy Patchies. The East Indian character of Babu was inspired by the immigration to the parish of Westmoreland of indentured laborers from India. Between 1834-1914 approximately 36,410 East Indians entered Jamaica.[4] The Captain and Flower Girl were costumed in "fancy dress" period fashion, with satin clothes, knee length pants, off-white stockings, ruffled jackets, white gloves, tennis shoes, and wire screen masks. Twenty-five Savanna-la-Mar troupe members participated in the 1951 competition. Most of the characters dressed in almost identical "fancy dress," and they represented characters whose counterparts can be found in British folk drama. These included a Father Christmas, a Barber, a Jockey, a Drunkard, a Sweeper, the Champion, and the Dukes of Essex and Warwick. When Martha Beckwith wrote about "Christmas Mummings" in the Jamaican parish of St. Elizabeth in 1923, she noted that the costumes were copied from Weldon's *Three Hundred and Fifty Ideas for Fancy Dress*, first published in London in 1917. Weldon and Company published pamphlets on fancy dress, fancy work, embroidery, etiquette, etc. during the period 1880s-1930s. It is quite possible that the Westmoreland troupes had access to similar books, but they are no longer used today.

Since all Jonkonnu troupes, regardless of their origin, wear wire screen masks, the masks serve as a good point of comparison. The Captain, Flower Girl, and the Pitchy Patchies from the Savanna-la-Mar troupe all had their masks painted in a similar manner. The mask itself was painted pink, the cheeks were red circles, and the lips were also red. The male masks had black moustaches and small black beards, and presumably the masks were designed to be read as recognizable Caucasian faces. In juxtaposition with this tradition, the masks of the troupe from Port Antonio, Portland are not designed to be seen as an identifiable type, least of all a Caucasian. The basic mask is left unpainted so that the brown or black skin shows through. The features are roughly painted, in dark colors and in a somewhat abstracted style. The eyes may be circles, shells, beads, or buttons. Often the nose is a simple straight line, and the cheeks are frequently covered with geometric patterns.

In contrast to the Savanna-la-Mar troupe, the Port Antonio troupe never wears "fancy dress." Their named characters and costume style more closely resemble the traditional, rural Jonkonnu type. When I saw them perform during the Christmas holidays of 1976, they included a cowhead, a warrior, a wild Indian, a devil, a policeman, and a "belly woman." All the costumes were embellished with pieces of mirrors, beads, paper cutouts, and feathers.

Although the Port Antonio and the Savanna-la-Mar groups differ in their choice of characters and their costumes, it is important to realize that both are considered Jonkonnu troupes by Jamaicans. What is of particular interest is to consider the heritage of these two types of Jonkonnu troupes.

The majority of eyewitness accounts of Jamaican Jonkonnu celebrations date from the period between 1800 and 1850. The few eighteenth-century accounts, except that of Edward Long, as already noted, mention animal costumes almost exclusively. By the beginning of the nineteenth century the Christmas parade seemed to have developed into an organized spectacle. An examination of about ten eyewitness accounts yields the following categories of performers: househeaddress performers, sets of females dressed in fine clothes, actor groups performing minidramas, kings and/or queens, mimic military men, musicians, Jacks-in-the-Green, occasional bulls or cow figures, and John Canoe. The identification of the John Canoe varies as these representative samples demonstrate:

> And they, (the sets), have always one or two Joncanoe men, smart youths fantastically dressed, and masked so as not be known.
>
> Alexander Barclay (1823)[5]

> The prominent character was, as usual, the John Canoe or Jack Pudding. He was a light, active, clean-made young Creole negro, without shoes or stockings; he wore a pair of light jean small clothes, all too wide, but confined at the knee, below and above, by bands of red tape . . . . He wore a splendid blue velvet waistcoat . . . . His coat was an old blue artillery uniform one, with a small bell hung to the extreme points of the swallow-tailed shirts . . . . He had an enormous cocked hat on, to which was appended in front a white false-face or mask . . . .
>
> Michael Scott (1833)[6]

> The John Canoe is a Merry Andrew dressed in a stripe doublet and bearing upon his head a kind of paste-board house-boat, filled with puppets, representing some sailors, other soldiers, others again slaves at work on a plantation.
>
> "Monk" Lewis (1816)[7]

In many accounts no separate John Canoe character is identified.

These nineteenth-century accounts reveal some interesting aspects of local Jonkonnu celebrations. In all the accounts the name "John Canoe" is applied, but the composition of the celebrations varied both chronologically and geographically. Nevertheless, all the reports discuss animal characters and grotesquely costumed performers which do not appear in later nineteenth-century reports, suggesting that Jonkonnu celebrations appeared to be increasingly more influenced by British artistic prototypes at the very time that the British influence was waning in the island. The white face masks are strong evidence of this.

This apparently paradoxical development might have been related to the issue of patronage of the festivals. All the reports of Jonkonnu that we have are written by white chroniclers who either lived on a plantation or in the towns, or were the guests of the local white residents. The reports, then, portray celebrations which were under the control of the white rural planter class or their urban commercial equivalents. For this reason we also get reports of white masters lending the blacks money to buy particular costumes, or even lending the costumes themselves. Hence, the costumes often reflected the tastes and the fashions of the patrons. Unfortunately, it seems that no visitor was bold enough to venture outside this patronized milieu to see whether the rural, peasant folk festivals retained stronger African elements than their European-sponsored urban and plantation counterparts.

In my research in Jamaica I found two distinct lines of opinion regarding the tradition of the present celebrations among my informants. One group claimed that the festivals had never ceased to be performed throughout the rural communities. Another group declared that the tradition had been interrupted from time to time, manifesting new syncretic forms with each resurrection. I am of the opinion, however, that both views are correct, to the extent that the rural celebrations did not have the publicity and hence the general recognition afforded the more European, more urban form. The 1951-52 celebrations brought both traditions together.

NASSAU

Contemporary Jamaican Jonkonnu celebrations demonstrate an important point: that these celebrations, their origin, and their characters differ in certain significant ways. Although the contemporary traditions are a flexible melange of many historical elements, these elements can be studied in order to better understand earlier historical accounts. A good case in point is the history of Junkanoo in Nassau, the Bahamas.

I will now attempt to establish the relationship between Nassau's Junkanoo and Jamaica's Jonkonnu. The *Nassau Guardian* has been publishing reports of Christmas and New Years' festivities for over a century. The earliest mention of the Christmas holiday season is in the December 24, 1864 edition. In a small editorial, the authors lament the fact that no Christmas pantomime is celebrated in Nassau. Seven years later, the December 27, 1871 edition mentions that the Grant's Town Band paraded on Christmas Day. (Grant's Town is the area of Nassau described as "over the hill," where the majority of black Bahamians have always resided.) The December 27, 1879 edition mentions that grotesquely dressed figures playing diverse instruments paraded. In the December 26, 1881, edition is a brief notice of a novel type of public Christmas celebration: A "van" filled with grotesque characters wearing horns and carrying horsewhips paraded down Bay Street. The December 26, 1883 edition notes that this same van and figures paraded again on Christmas, although this time they were accompanied by the Grant's Town Drummers and Fifers.

These scattered references infer that the performers and musicians who paraded on Christmas Day were blacks celebrating Christmas according to their own traditions. They had come from "over the hill" to parade on Bay Street, the main street of then white Nassau. According to the white newspaper correspondents, the blacks were dressed in a grotesque manner. Since these same correspondents presumably never ventured "over the hill," there are unfortunately no reports on Christmas celebrations, or any type of celebration, in Grant's Town itself. In addition, no explanation is offered why, in the 1860s or 1870s, blacks from "over the hill" began parading on Bay Street.

An intriguing article in the December 25, 1875 *Nassau Guardian* unconsciously juxtaposes the blacks' style of Christmas celebration with the white one. At a white Nassau grammar school the students performed a Christmas masquerade. They did a burlesque of St. George and the Dragon, which included the characters of Maid Marian, the Turkish Knight, the Grand Master, etc. Unfortunately the article does not go into more detail. Yet it does offer a clue to the development of a British folk drama tradition among blacks in the Caribbean. School children performing British mummers plays could have served as a means of transmitting costumes and characters to the black population. Roger Abrahams has described these same plays as performed by blacks in St. Kitts,[8] yet there is no mention of Bahamian blacks performing these dramas in the nineteenth century.

It seems that whites never participated in the festivities on Bay Street as performers. Newspaper reports describe white Bahamians' Christmas Holiday as spent strolling on Bay Street and attending choir recitals and dances at the Nassau hotels.

Throughout the latter 1880s the *Nassau Guardian* reported an increase in the number of fife and drum bands and masqueraders parading on Bay Street on Christmas Day. By 1889 the reporters' accounts were only slightly more detailed as they mention masqueraders performing tricks. In 1901 they reported that the masqueraders from Grant's Town were out in great numbers, dressed in strange costumes and wearing masks. More complete descriptions of the costumes were not given. One can only assume that the festivities "over the hill" had always been strong and that, with increased tolerance and receptivity at the turn of the century, more and more blacks were parading on Bay Street. Interestingly, this annual parade is never given a name.

During a 1976 interview, Charles Storr, then eighty-five years old, recalled the celebrations at the turn of the century. His father used to take him down to the market on Bay Street where the Junkanoo performed. He remembers men parading on stilts and others who wore sponge costumes. (Sponge costumes were popular in the 1920s and 1930s before the supply of sponges was exhausted.)

Another Bahamian, Hubert McKinney, ninety years old in 1976, recalls that the stilt dancers walked around town and collected money for their performances. He stated that the most famous stilt men were from Haiti: "They came here to take money . . . you could tell they were from Haiti by their speech. . . you could hear it a mile away."

In the early 1920s the increasing numbers of masqueraders came into conflict with local authorities. The Christmas festivities on Bay Street were banned in 1922, although a *Nassau Guardian* article of that year reports that there was a good deal of merrymaking "over the hill." In 1923, the masqueraders remained over the hill in protest of the preceding year's regulations.

On December 27, 1924 the *Nassau Guardian* reported that the "John Canoes and dancers" came out in large numbers. This is the first official occasion that I have been able to document when the name "John Canoe" is applied to the Christmas celebration in Nassau. Of note is the spelling: it is the same as that used in the nineteenth century in Jamaica. Although no proof exists, it would seem that Christmas masquerading was practiced in Nassau and the name "John Canoe" was applied to the practice, *ex post facto*, by someone who knew of the well-publicized Jamaican tradition.

By the late 1920s John Canoe was quite popular with Bahamians. A December 28, 1927 *Nassau Guardian* article reported that visitors, eager to see John Canoe, had flocked into Nassau and that, due to popular acclaim, another parade would be held on January 2.

By piecing together scattered sources from the early twentieth century, one can begin to visualize what these Bahamian "John Canoes" actually looked like. Alan Parsons notes that the Christmas performers were blacks wearing white masks or whitened faces.[9] Their costumes were either borrowed from Shakespearian models or were made from burlap bags decorated with odds and ends. Robert Curry notes that these same performers were all masked and covered their bodies with shredded strips of colored paper.[10] This reference is important since it is one of the first written descriptions of the costume type that indicated the origins for contemporary costumes. The current costumes are made from crepe paper (imported from the United States), hand sheared to achieve a layered fringed effect.

Amelia Defries' 1929 description is one of the most complete, noting that most men were dressed in knee-length skirts with their legs covered by light-colored tights.[11] Many wore British-style safari hats and all wore machine-made masks in imitation of whites. Other incidental costumes included a man in a loose fitting polka dotted clown suit and another covered from head to foot in shredded paper or cloth and wearing a tall pointed cap. Defries indicates that all the masqueraders were divided into bands representing various over the hill neighborhoods. The leaders danced with a "one step forward and two steps back" pattern; a step which is still considered the appropriate Junkanoo dance step. These dancers were accompanied by musicians playing small, open-ended drums covered with a taut skin. Defries comments that "you might walk the length of the street (Bay Street) and from end to end you would hear no variation in the rhythm."

These descriptions pinpoint certain important particulars. Black masqueraders were often costumed in imitation of British dress and wore white face masks. A large contingent, however, wore burlap bags decorated with odds and ends or wore shredded paper costumes. Some of these characters also powdered their faces with flour or wore white face masks. There is no mention of the collecting of money, of characters with particular names, or of animal characters. All former Junkanoo participants whom I interviewed agreed that performers never acted out dramas or played a specific role.

Except for certain similarities in costume based on a British prototype, the history of the Nassau Christmas celebration is, in essence, very different from that of Jamaican Jonkonnu. The use of the term Junkanoo by Bahamian officials seems to have been adopted for publicity purposes, most probably by people aware of the literature on the Jamaican festival, and the Bahamian festival is largely a Tourist Board promotion nowadays.

By the 1930s the administration of Nassau's "Johnny Canoe Parade" was in the hands of the Development Board and it was held on New Year's Day in order to placate those, including the staff of the *Nassau Guardian*, who felt that a raucous parade was an inappropriate way to celebrate Christmas Day. The Development Board offered cash prizes for original costumes and also took over some of the artistic direction of the parade. As reported in the *Nassau Guardian* January 2, 1934: "the mummers heads which had been specially imported . . . for the occasion were very effective." These included a John Bull, a wolf, a deathshead, and Pierrot. Top prizes in 1934 were awarded to an Old and New Year duo, a bird, a watertower, a porcupine, and two ships. Certainly, the style and character of the celebration had changed since a "van filled with grotesque figures" had careened down Bay Street in the 1880s. By 1939 a separate John Canoe Committee was formed in order to deal with increased participation in and popularity of the parade.

The more recent history of Nassau's Junkanoo is not of immediate concern. Public Junkanoo celebrations were discontinued during the 1940s and only officially revived in 1956. Today Nassau's Junkanoo rivals Trinidad's Carnival in scope and organization. The bands are divided into themes; the costumes are all made from fringed crepe paper; and the first prize is often as much as $1,000.

BERMUDA, THE LEEWARD ISLANDS, AND BELIZE

In Bermuda the Christmas dancers and their celebration are known as Gombey. Although they traditionally appeared on Christmas, they too now perform on Boxing Day. These gaily costumed street dancers have performed since at least the early 1800s, although the style of their costumes and the festival's formal structure have changed considerably.

In an early account, Susette Lloyd recorded an 1829 Christmas celebration performed on the lawn of an estate where she was a visitor.[12] She does not give the festivity a special name. She desribed the participants as singing special songs, and covering their clothing with scarlet cloth decorated with colored ribbons. Some of the dancers also used paint on their bodies. The musicians wore neat white uniforms with scarlet facings.

An editorial in the *Bermuda Royal Gazette* a few years later, on December 26, 1837, claimed that "the savage and nonsensical exhibition of the Gomba, practised here by the idle, should be done away with as a thing not suited to a civilized community, and highly dangerous to Passengers on horses or in carriages." While this editorial does not describe the festival specifically, it does imply that the "Gomba" was practiced outdoors and most probably took the form of a perambulatory event in which costumed individuals participated. It is possible that Lloyd's description is also of a Gomba festival.

Nineteenth-century documentation on the festival's form and costumes is sketchy. Individual groups of black Bermudans staged local performances in their own distinct manner. One element, however, seems to have been consistent among the various performances: the use of a particular headdress . . . a house worn on the head. Theodore Godet reports a Christmas parade whose participants sang songs of ridicule and derision.[13] The chief instrument was a small barrel drum called a gomby. The participants wore masks, fantastic costumes, and a "chateaux on their heads." H. Carrington Bolton's 1890 article, however, is the most thorough:

> The gomby parade is usually held on Christmas Eve, between 11 P.M. and 2 A.M.; perhaps it has been transferred to the holiday season because greater leisure is enjoyed, and it is a time of general merrymaking. At this time groups of men and boys (women seldom take part) parade about the country, going from house to house singing, dancing, and playing on rude musical instruments, among which the triangle and tambourine are prominent, penny whistles and concertinas being also called to their aid. The men wear their ordinary garments, but are masked, bearing on their heads the heads and horns of hideous looking beasts (formidable only to an uncultured mind), as well as beautifully made imitations of houses and ships, both lighted by candles. . . .[14]

Bertha March, writing in 1929, described a Christmas Eve event where the Afro-Bermudians danced on the veranda to the music of an old accordion. "One had a strange little house, with lighted candles inside, perched upon his head. . . ."[15]

In the 1930s the *Bermudian* magazine began publishing a series of articles on the Gombeys. E. C. McLaughlin's 1932 *Bermudian* article stated that by the turn of the century the Gombey's costume consisted of "models of houses or full-rigged sips skillfully made of wood, cardboard, and coloured paper, lighted from within by a candle."[16] These models fully enveloped the head. Prior to this the Gombey dancers were often dressed in "hideous masks and haphazard splatterings of war paint." McLaughlin offers no documentation in support of this chronological scheme.

On October 22, 1976, I interviewed Dr. Kenneth Robinson, former Gombey participant and retired Chief Education Officer. He had joined Gombey as a young boy, after hearing his father tell stories of the festival. Recalling one such story, he described a dance group that carried illuminated houses on their heads. Dr. Robinson himself had never seen this, but his father remembered it from the turn of the century. Charles Place, Sr., another former Gombey dancer, had heard stories of a group that wore a box on the head and said that "at that time they used to light it up."

Since Mclaughlin's 1932 article is illustrated, it is unfortunate that he does not comment further on his own photographs. None of the Gombeys photographed wear costumes that match any earlier historical description. By 1932 the visual form of the celebration seems to have undergone a metamorphosis. The most likely explanation is supplied by one of McLaughlin's captions, "Modern Gombeys unlike those of the Nineteenth Century who were Bermuda born, those of today are almost exclusively immigrants from the West Indies."[17]

Interestingly, the Gombeys in these 1932 photographs are dressed almost exactly like those of the 1970s. Their capes and trousers are covered with beads, sequins, pieces of mirror, ribbons, bells, and fringes. The 1932 photographs showed white face masks while today the masks are made of wire screen with painted pink cheeks and red lips. These headdresses, trimmed with glitter and tall peacock feathers, about four feet tall, have been the Gombey's costume since at least the 1930s, but hardly earlier than that.

The suggestion that this costume is not indigenous to Bermuda is further supported by all informants. Charles Place, an informant I interviewed in 1976 stated flatly, "I know for a fact that it didn't begin here. . . .It comes from down in the Caribbean." A 1948 report from St. Davids, Bermuda, by E. A. McCallan states:

> At this season (Christmas) the gombeys came up from the East End to amuse us and collect pennies. They were the real thing, and not the exotic from the West Indies now accepted by the uninformed as the Bermuda articles. These island gombeys of my youth wore no uniform or fancy dress, they appeared only after sunset, and their chief, if not only, properties were an improvised drum and an illuminated tissue paper-and-frame-house on the head of the most active member of the band who danced and pranced while the others sang.[18]

The Bermuda Gombeys, unlike Christmas masqueraders from other islands, sang while performing. A comparison of a song recorded in 1890 and one from 1932 yields some interesting information. H. Carrington Bolton collected a number of Gombey songs, and the refrain in one refers to one Simon Taylor.[19] The archivist at the Bermuda Library claims that Taylor is not and was not a traditional Bermuda name. The tune is reminiscent of a sea shanty. It makes reference to a "ribber," a geographical feature unheard of in Bermuda. I quote the words in part:

> Oh turn that house upside down,
>   Simon Taylor, high-lo,
> Hy-lo, and away we go,
>   Simon Taylor, hy-lo,
> I'm gwine down de ribber to get some shads,
>   Simon Taylor, hy-lo.
> Mamie, mamie, give me some bread,
>   Simon Taylor, hy-lo.

Both Bolton (1890) and McLaughlin (1932) quote the same verse dealing with competition between the parishes of Bermuda:

> Paget girls are pretty girls.
>   Simon Taylor high-low.
> Warwick girls are ugly girls,
>   Simon Taylor high-low.
> Warwick girls aint got no hair,
>   Simon Taylor high-low.
> Take a bit o'wool and stick it dere,
>   Simon Taylor high-low.

It is not unlikely that many Gombey elements were introduced into the Bermudan festival during the latter part of the nineteenth century. As an island, Bermuda's outside contacts and maritime trade brought a number of black Bermudans an awareness of the wider Caribbean area. As early as 1733, 150 Afro-Bermudan slaves manned the island's sixty sloops which handled the greater portion of local commerce. As the trade expanded, even more of the local blacks traveled abroad as sailors.

The immigration of the 1920s probably had a pronounced impact on the festivals, as an ever increasing number of laborers came to Bermuda from the islands of St. Kitts, Nevis, and Antigua. Indeed, in 1930 the Registrar General of the island reported that "as usual, the largest number of parents of non-Bermudian origin came from St. Kitts-Nevis." In an interview published in 1946 in the *Bermudian* magazine, Charles Norford, the leader of one of the most prominent Gombey groups admitted that he came from St. Kitts in 1922.

This St. Kitts-Nevis connection is related to the folk festivals of the Leeward and Windward Islands. The Christmas masquerades of both islands are similar. As early as 1896, Alfred Williams collected and published a number of texts and costume descriptions of the local masquerades.[20] Not surprisingly, in view of the findings for Jamaica, the texts are marvelous adaptions of English folk plays, especially the David and Goliath dramas. The performers included "Indians with feathered and horn headdresses, tomahawk and leggings . . . British sailors, and minstrels." There were also men on stilts and others in "grotesque costumes."

A December 25, 1908 description of the festival in Russell's Rest, just outside of Charlestown, Nevis helps confirm the possibility of the Bermuda connection. It is taken from Antonia Williams's scrapbook:

> One man came dressed either as a devil or a monkey led by chain, and some other men in white masks and head dresses of peacocks' feathers about three feet high, and their clothes sewn all over with penny glasses and postcards, and any other tinsel. The dance was a mixture of quadrille, lancer, and war dance . . . very funny. The singing was discordant . . . the instruments, a drum and various they had made themselves.[21]

Happily Miss Williams was an amateur photographer, and her snapshots may prove to be the earliest extant visual evidence of these Christmas festivals. In one photograph a group of masqueraders are assembled around a "May Pole." The men dressed as women wear a simple cloth dress and a long white apron which is decorated with bangles. The male costume is all white: close fitting shirt and leggings with a knee length skirt worn over layers of fringe. Some of the men wear mock military uniforms with ribbons which criss-cross over their chests. Both types of costume include cloth head wraps and screen masks painted white. The male masks include a thin moustache.

Some of these costume elements are found not only in Bermudan Gombey, but also in Belizean John Canoe. The history of Belizean John Canoe is beyond the scope of the present inquiry, but certain factors are of direct relevance to this study. The costumes worn by the Belizean John Canoe participants in the *Carifesta* July 1976 celebrations in Jamaica resemble those described previously in Bermuda and Nevis. Tall peacock feathers were mounted on a pill-box type hat decorated with colored pompoms and worn over a head wrap. The white wire screen masks had Caucasian features complete with thin black moustaches. The dancers wore white knee-length trousers and white long sleeve shirts. In mock military fashion, ribbons criss-crossed over the chest. This basic costume is also being worn in a photo of Carib John Canoe performers from the early 1900s, published by Robert Dirks and Virginia Kearns in *National Studies*, 1975.[22]

There does seem to be a consistency of costume elements which hint at cultural linkages between various Caribbean islands. At least two possible explanations are suggested. One is that these costumes derive from a single island source. The other is that simultaneous parallel structures developed, derived from a common British source. The white mock military uniform and white face mask support the latter viewpoint. Yet, how does one explain the parallel development of the identical tall peacock headdress? The concept that all the festivals are related through British colonialism is not unreasonable given the substantial trade and commerce that occurred among the British islands. Ships carried more than consumer commodities.

Perhaps Jamaica acted as the intermediary for the areas under discussion. It was certainly the largest and most important of all English Caribbean colonies, except British Guiana. Yet Beckwith supplies the only description of Jamaican celebrations between 1900 and 1950, and she does not mention any costumes which fit the above descriptions. Since contemporary Jamaican Masquerade (as distinct from Jonkonnu) demonstrates British influence, it does not seem unreasonable to assume that this tradition was extant in Jamaica during the period for which we have no information.

Older chronicles of the Christmas festivals make frequent reference to a particular type of costume headdress. This headdress, imitation houses and ships worn by the festival dancers, is documented in early accounts. Only later is the British masquerade type mentioned. The house and ship headdresses, however, continued to be noticed among the British masquerade types.

One of the essential characteristics of the older, more traditional, Bermuda Gombeys, was the carrying of illuminated models of houses and ships. These cardboard and wooden models were covered with tissue paper. Although Godet (1860) mentions these, a more complete description is from Bolton (1890):

> The men wear their ordinary garments, but are masked, bearing on their heads the heads and horns of hideous-looking beasts (formidable only to an uncultured mind), as well as beautifully made imitations of houses and ships, both lighted by candles. The houses are known as gombay houses, and are large enough to admit the head of the bearer inserted through a hole below, the building resting on his shoulders. These are more common than the ships, which are fully rigged.[23]

Certainly the wearing of the "heads and horns of hideous beasts" is not derived from British masquerade and, as far as I can determine, neither is the wearing of illuminated houses and ships. Chroniclers of Bermuda festivals describe these houses and ships through the 1940s, although they are no longer used in Bermuda Gombey.

In Jamaica, there are many references to the wearing of a frame house or ship during Jonkonnu performances. The earliest report is in Monk Lewis, cited earlier. Cynric Williams (1826) stated that the house itself was known as Jonkanoo. Belisario (1837) even published a colored drawing of a John Canoe dancer with white face mask, wig, military jacket, and carrying on his head a frame house covered with mirrors, tinsel, colored paper, and pompoms. Monk (1834) and Waddell (1863) also mention these houses.

The most recent description of this practice comes from Beckwith (1923). She witnessed two Jonkonnu performances, one in Lacovia, St. Elizabeth and the other in Prospect, Manchester. During both performances, the dancers wore house headdresses. The one from Lacovia is described by Beckwith as follows:

> his cap, which stood fully four feet high was two-storied, with four pil-lared porticoes at right angles to each other. . . . He slipped the house over his head, resting it against his shoulders behind and balancing it with cords held in his hands. . . .[24]

This description resembles Bolton's so closely that one begins to suspect that both refer to the same tradition. No evidence exists for the use of this style of headdress in either the 1951 or 1952 Jamaican Jonkonnu competitions and none are used today.

I did not locate any written references to the wearing of a house headdress in Nassau's Junkanoo celebrations. Curry (1928) mentions that the dancers wore colored paper cut into shreds and a headdress which often took the form of a ship, which was also covered with shredded paper. Charles Storr, in a 1976 interview, agreed that during the 1920s and 1930s performers often were costumed with two-masted sailing boats on their heads. By the late 1930s prizes were being awarded and ship costumes were often mentioned as winners. A 1941 Development Board photograph shows a masquerader who resembles Curry's 1928 description quite closely, and might have been a prototype. It is difficult to determine whether these scanty references establish a connection between the Bermuda and Jamaica practices, and the wearing of a ship headdress in the Nassau parades. Hubert McKinney, a ninety-year-old Bahamian stated in an interview on October 29, 1976 that the wearing of imitation ships was a relatively recent introduction to the Junkanoo and that he could not remember such costumes at any earlier period.

The historical links which spread the common Christmas festivals around the Caribbean cannot be established firmly beyond the equal experiences of European colonialism. Nevertheless, the tradition of wearing illuminated houses or ships on the head could be just as easily Caribbean, African, or European.

On a recent trip to Haiti, I discovered a small tissue-paper frame house in the ethnographic museum. The representation, a child's toy called *fanal*, was carried around during the Christmas celebrations when adults were expected to reward the children with monetary contributions for their effort. *Fanal*, however, is not a native Haitian festival. It is also celebrated in Senegambia and parts of Sierra Leone. In the latter region, Professor David Gamble has documented a *fanal* celebration coinciding with the Islamic holiday of Ramadan, the ninth holy month. The earliest African references to *fanal* are from Gorée, Senegal, while other such celebrations are documented for St. Louis (Senegal) and Banjul, Gambia, reputed to have the largest and best-known *fanal* festivities.

Everywhere the *fanal* has a wooden frame covered with paper, cut in elaborate patterns often resembling fine filigree. *Fanales* vary in size from one to twenty feet in length, and are carried during processions. At night interior candles provide illumination. Most *fanales* take the form of sailing ships, although many are representative of dwelling houses. Indeed, a recent development in the construction of *fanales* is to portray airplanes, motorcars, and mosques. *Fanal* processions which take place throughout Christmas Eve are a polite form of solicitations.

There is no established connection between the Haitian and Senegambian forms of *fanal*. More research needs to be done on the origin of the Senegambian *fanal* festival, especially to ascertain why a common European romance nomenclature should have appeared along the West African coast in a local folk festival. The *fanal* itself closely resembles the paper lanterns commonly found in Western Europe. When one considers that the first written reference currently available of this householddress comes from Jamaica, it is not unlikely that the custom may have travelled from Jamaica to Senegambia. The links between Africa and the Caribbean, especially in forms of culture, were not unilaterally from east to west.

What can be ascertained, then, is that the Caribbean formed a catalyst for the merging of European and African traditions. The Jamaican Jonkonnu festival reflects the junction of these two traditions of folk culture. The African elements are most obvious in the characters of cowhead and horsehead, and an African-Creole aesthetic is demonstrated by the choice of costume and by the decoration of the masks of such common characters such as the warriors and the Indians. Moreover, the supporting music and the performance styles also reflect much of the African heritage in the Caribbean. The prevalence of the householddress in such diverse places as Senegambia, Haiti, Jamaica, Bermuda, and the Bahamas demonstrates the breadth and complexity of the contacts through time and space.

British colonialism in general and individual European patronage helped spread the elements of the English folk activities throughout those parts of the Atlantic World where the English proprietary classes settled or sojourned. In the Caribbean, this English influence is most obvious in the white face masks and the imitation of English court and military characters. Moreover, the English were probably most responsible for the distinction between "fancy dress" characters and those wearing burlap sacks decorated with the scraps of cloth represented by Pitchy Patchy.

However clear the themes of these festivals may be, the task of establishing the origins and interconnections is extremely great. Culture changes with each society, and within each stratum of each society. Caribbean society has a long history of being both stratified and changing. The Jamaican Jonkonnu, the earliest of the folk festivals, was much advertised during the nineteenth century when many visitors to the island published their travel accounts. This publicity attracted imitation, even while the original Jamaican festivals themselves were undergoing change. The Jonkonnu festivals in Jamaica influenced the Nassau Junkanno parades, although not nearly as strongly as did local political control and local Bahamian patronage. In contrast, due to direct historical links, the festivals in Bermuda, St. Kitts, Nevis, and Belize include traditions which interrrelate closely with one another as well as with Jamaica.

NOTES

The research for this paper was carried out in 1976. I wish to thank the following informants who kindly agreed to interviews: Hubert Kinney and Charles Storr of Nassau, The Bahamas; Charles Place and Dr. Kenneth Robinson of Hamilton, Bermuda; Cooper and Jim Robinson of Westmoreland Parish, Jamaica, and Theodore Sealy and Ranny Williams of Kingston, Jamaica. I'm also grateful to the staff of the Institute of Jamaica, and especially Cheryl Ryman, dance researcher of the African-Caribbean Institute, Kingston, Jamaica.

1. Kwame Yeba Daaku, *Trade and Politics on the Gold Coast 1600-1720* (Oxford, 1970).

2. Frederick G. Cassidy, *Dictionary of Jamaican English* (Cambridge, 1970); Judith Bettelheim, "The Jonkonnu Festival," *Jamaica Journal*, 10 (1976): 20-27.

3. See Bettelheim, "Jonkonnu Festival."

4. Rex Nettleford, *Mirror, Mirror* (Kingston, 1970).

5. Alexander Barclay, *A Practical View of the Present State of Slavery* (London, 1823), p. 11.

6. Michael Scott, *Tom Cringle's Log* (London, 1833), pp. 247-48.

7. M. G. Lewis, *Journal of a West Indian Proprietor* (London, 1863), p. 51.

8. Roger Abrahams, "Pull Out Your Purse and Pay," *Folklore* 79 (1968): 176-201.

9. Alan Parsons, *A Winter in Paradise* (London, 1926).

10. Robert Curry, *Bahamian Lore* (Paris, 1928).

11. Amelia Defries, *The Fortunate Islands* (London, 1929), p. 46.

12. Susette H. Lloyd, *Sketches of Bermuda* (London, 1835).

13. Theodore Godet, *Bermuda* (London, 1860).

14. H. Carrington Bolton, "Gombay: A Festival Rite of Bermudian Negroes," *Journal of American Folklore,* 3 (1890): 222-23.

15. Bertha March, *Bermuda Days* (London, 1929), p. 29.

16. E. C. McLaughlin, "Gombeys and Casave Pie," *The Bermudian* (December 1932), p. 8.

17. Ibid.

18. E. A. McCallan, *Life in Old St. Davids* (Bermuda, 1948), p. 174.

19. Bolton, "Gombay," p. 225.

20. Alfred Williams, "A Miracle Play in the West Indies." *Journal of American Folklore* 33 (1896): 117-20

21. Antonia Williams, *A Tour Through the West Indies* Mss., University of West Indies, Mona, collection.

22. Robert Dirks and Virginia Kearns, *National Studies*, 3, no. 6 (1975): 1-15.

23. Bolton, "Gombay," p. 223.

24. Martha Beckwith, *Christmas Mummings in Jamaica* (New York, 1923), p. 10.

Checkout Receipt

Delta College Library
02/11/10 12:02PM
****

---

rica and the Caribbean : the legacies of a link /
einv2
ALL NO: F2169 .A37 1979
1434000890065 03/04/10
UE TIME

OTAL: 1

6

THE AFRICAN IMPACT
ON LANGUAGE AND LITERATURE
IN THE ENGLISH-SPEAKING CARIBBEAN

Maureen Warner Lewis

CONTINUED EXISTENCE OF AFRICAN LANGUAGES:
A CASE STUDY OF YORUBA IN TRINIDAD

It has hardly been realized that African languages are still spoken and used
in the American hemisphere. Research in this linguistic area has been ham-
pered by intellectual skepticism, racial prejudice, and the lack of African
language expertise in the local communities to identify and record these
languages. The unfortunate result of these deficiencies is that before the
awareness of, and interest in, this phenomenon can be fully stimulated,
African speech and cultural communities will have been lost or dispersed
through death and through social and industrial development. There have
been helpful contributions on Yoruba and other African languages in Cuba,[1]
and Twi lexical items in Jamaica's Maroon speech have already been in-
vestigated.[2] Between 1966-72 I have located Yoruba, Kikongo, Hausa, Fon,
and Arabic speakers in Trinidad; and in 1972 Nago (Yoruba), Kikongo, and
Mahi speakers in Jamaica. Apart from Twi elements which have persisted
over four centuries, the other languages have a separation in time from their
mainland matrices of no more than a century and a half. For this reason,
the languages other than Twi persist not only as lexical items, but are articulated by their speakers with varying levels of syntactic competence and
sophistication.

Introduction into the British West Indies of indentured Africans in the nineteenth century is responsible for this short time-depth. After the British Parliament's abolition of the slave trade in 1809, slaves liberated by British naval patrols off the West African coast were often encouraged or forced into indenture. The majority of slaves at that time were Yoruba, Kongo and Hausa. The period of the most intensive introduction of African indentured labor into Trinidad was 1840-60.[3]

Twentieth-century speakers of Yoruba in Trinidad are the rear-guard survivors of tribal communities which existed on the island during the last century. By the time Yoruba had filtered down to the second generation its tonal differentiations had either become subjected to patterns of Trinidad English and French Creole intonation, or were only partially retained. Where tonal distinctions are still scrupulously maintained, they sometimes tend to be exaggeratedly higher or lower than pitch levels acceptable in contemporary Yoruba in Nigeria. Non-Yoruba phones derived from French Creole and English rarely enter the phonology, and in one instance the stress and syllable timing of Hindi.[4] A few lexical items from French Creole and English have also been borrowed. Most phonological changes are systematic, but some idiolects display a fair degree of unsystematic consonantal shifts.[5] In sentences generated by the speakers, syntactic analysis reveals a simplification of the verb phrase to its stem[6] and omission or reduction of other syntactic categories. In some instances, English word order and idioms derived from English Creole as well as from Spanish are used as a model for translation. Such interference is particularly noticeable where the speaker is literate in English.

These observations reflect on the fact that African languages exist in a symbiotic relationship with Indo-European languages with which they have come into contact in the Caribbean: because they once participated in a creative creolizing fusion they have bequeathed features to languages with a different lexical base. African languages, however, have outlived that initial process and have in turn reabsorbed features from European languages and from the very Creoles that they have fathered.

AFRICAN LANGUAGE USE

A survey of Yoruba language use in the nineteenth century further indicates the impact of African languages on the culture and psychology of Caribbean peoples.[7] The picture that emerges indicates ambivalent attitudes of resentment and accomodation including the pragmatic concession of an immigrant people to objective social reality, and at the same time, faith in mystical redemption from an alien law and social environment.

Yoruba was the language of in-group communication, but since the immigrants spoke various dialects of Yoruba, dialect-switching aided communication, and no doubt increased as each new generation was born into a more complex dialectal community. While this dialectally heterogeneous Yoruba remained the in-group language, it is clear that French Creole also began to usurp this domestic role. This phenomenon certainly reflects increasing pressure on the African minority to conform to creole social norms. The African community was itself fragmented along linguistic and cultural lines, and since the colony's *lingua franca* was French Creole, Africans had little choice but to meet the out-group on the latter's common ground.

Living a peasant existence in scattered semiisolated tribal communities, or in cosmopolitan urban ghettos, nineteenth-century Africans had little need of English, the official language, except in rare instances such as when they encountered the law. Disadvantaged by demographic location, by economic and linguistic status, many Africans tried to convert their liabilities to advantages. They maintained mutual-aid tribal associations to foster their cultural heritage and to derive economic and death benefits. By adopting Christianity they demonstrated to the society at large a willingness to conform on a crucial public issue and therefore eased the emotional burden of their social ostracism. This ostracism was caused as much by their language as by their dress and tribal body marks. Becoming Christian did not, however, mean total severance from their own traditional worship and they continued to serve their deities under Catholic saints' names. Just as the saints carried a European label, they also carried a secret identity under a Yoruba name. Hence, St. Michael the Archangel was in fact Ogun. He had performed the same function in the Christian Heaven as in their ancestral home. He stood at the gates of Heaven with a flaming sword; Ogun was the pioneer who opened the pathway for the gods to visit mankind on earth—he did this by discovering the metal, iron, with which he forged an axe to hew through the forest. So he was not two identities, but one. In the same way, Africans themselves carried two identities. Prohibited by public sanction from carrying indigenous names, the same person officially known as Christiana Williams, for instance, was also known in the Yoruba community as Osuntoki, daughter of Efulabo.

Language was therefore a powerful tool of in-group identification. And since it was not understood by the society at large, it became a secret code. They abused the police in it, they warned each other against police raids, they pleaded their cause before God for redemption from "the sons of the whites who brought us here." "Every dog must have his day," they warned.

K'a maa wo
K'a maa w'oriṣa
B'oyinbo l'oke
Ọlọpa b'ọtun
Ṣeṣa maa wo
Abẹlubẹ wọn ṣe

Caught between *oyinbo* (the whites—rulers) and *ọlọpa* (police—agents of the rulers), they looked to the *oriṣa* (deities, saints) for their survival. In their own language, they complained of what they considered slave labor, and of paltry wages. They saw their own children alienated from them, born as they were under the white man's flag, and growing up amid strange languages and customs. To them, their children had been born into slavery. All these emotions of bitterness were given vent in their own tongue.

Cornered like this, their deepest prayers and desires were expressed through their mother tongue. It was, and still is, explicitly stated that Yoruba is more "powerful" than a European language. So grandparents blessed their grandchildren on Christmas day with Yoruba prayers. Morning and evening prayers for safety and success were uttered in Yoruba. The dead needed Yoruba songs to despatch them properly. Animal sacrifices during religious ceremonies were accompanied by chants and salutations with ancient esoteric references. Hundreds of chants praising the *oriṣa* were retained, and are still used by Trinidadians who today continue to worship them. In addition to this formidable number of *oriṣa* chants, the Yoruba have also contributed dirges and secular songs, some of which carry historical references to the wars and social upheavels in Yorubaland in the nineteenth century.

THE CREOLES

In both the English- and French-speaking Caribbean, the dominant, though unofficial, languages are Creoles. Scholarship regarding the Creoles first focused on theories of their origin. A heated debate has centered around this issue and the debate is not yet over.[8] Discussion also focused on the continuum phenomenon—variations in the extent to which Creole speech approximated to its lexical European model. These speech variations are now defined as "basilect" when Creole is furthest from its model, "mesolect"—a median position on the continuum scale, and "acrolect"—speech closely approximating to, but yet not identifiable with, the model.

Since the first Creole scholars were native European language speakers, greatest attention was paid to the peculiarities of the basilect which featured speech forms most at variance with European usage. The increase in linguistic descriptions of African languages over the last three decades has however led to a revision of the role ascribed to African languages in the formation of Creoles. First, there came a growing awareness of Africanisms of a lexical nature still retained in Creoles. Today, the search to identify the African impact on these languages extends beyond lexis. Where formerly one was able to describe Creole languages only in terms of Indo-European structures, interest has now shifted to assessing the important heritage bequeathed by West African tongues to Creole syntactic collocations, conceptual categories, residual tonal features and intonation, unstressing, and syllable structure.[9] These findings have in turn allowed new insights into the problematic question of Creole origins.

AFRICAN IDIOMATIC EXPRESSION IN CREOLES

By confining our comparison to Yoruba and Trinidad Creole English, we can trace the provenance of a few idioms and concepts in the latter, without denying the parallel occurrence of such idioms in other West African languages as well.

Yoruba: Enia ni.
Literal translation: Human being he is.
Trinidad English: He is people (too).
Gloss: An assertion of humanity. The individual is worthy of regard.

Yoruba: Ori ẹ o da.
Literal translation: Head your not good.
Trinidad English: You mad/doting.

Yoruba: Ṣe kia.
Literal translation: Do quickly.
Trinidad English: Do quick.
Gloss: Hurry.

Yoruba: O ya!
Literal translation: It is quick/alive.
Trinidad English: O ya!
Gloss: "Let's go!" Exclamation used up till the 1960s by bandleaders or singers whenever music or a calypso was about to begin.

Yoruba: Ohunkohun.
Literal translation: Thing + connective + thing.

Trinidad English: T'ing and t'ing.
Gloss: . . . and so on and so forth.

Yoruba: . . . kini.
Literal translation: thing.
Trinidad English: the . . . t'ing . . . .
Gloss: the . . . what's it? I can't remember.

Yoruba: Ki l'o ṣe e?
Literal translation: What is it does/grieves you?
Trinidad English: What do you?
Gloss: What's wrong?

Yoruba: L'ọjọ oni.
Literal translation: In day today.
Trinidad English: Today day.
Gloss: Emphatic.

Yoruba: Otutu mu mi.
Literal translation: Cold took/held me.
Trinidad English: (The) cold take/have me.
Gloss: I have the cold.

Yoruba: N'igba gbogbo.
Literal translation: In time all.
Trinidad English: All time.
Gloss: Always.

Yoruba: Mo jẹ tan.
Literal translation: I ate finish.
Trinidad English: I done eat.

Yoruba: O fọ ọwọ.
Literal translation: He washed hand.
Trinidad English: He wash hand.
Gloss: Syntactic form used in a recital of actions: "He
                       wash hand, he wash head . . . ."

Yoruba: Fi omi si igi.
Literal translation: Put water to plant.
Trinidad English: Put water to the plant.
Gloss: Water the plant.

Yoruba: Kuro n'ibẹ.
Literal translation: Come out in there.
Trinidad English: Come out in there.
Gloss: Come out of there.

Yoruba:	Sọ ọrọ buruku.
Literal translation:	Speak word bad.
Trinidad English:	Bad talk.
Gloss:	Speak evil of/speak in a deprecating way about.

Yoruba:	Joko sibẹ!
Literal translation:	Sit to there.
Trinidad English:	You stay there!
Gloss:	You're foolish enough not to believe me.

Linguistic correspondences can be traced even further. The pace, idiom, phrase length, and sequence of mood in the following quarrel, extracted from a popular printed serial in Western Nigeria in 1975, bears striking similarities with Creole expression.

Yoruba	*Trinidad Creole English*
Emi lo mbu?	Is me you 'busing?
Mo bu ẹ niyẹn. Kil'o fẹ ṣe fun Mi? Iya aje!	Yes, I with you self. What you have with me. You witch!
Maa kuku f'ejo ẹ sun iya ẹ na!	I footee report you to your mother, nuh.
Ẹ gbọ iya were yi t'o mbu iya mi!	Hear this mad woman 'busing my mother!
Ọrọ lo fẹ gbọ. O o si by'ọrọ naa. Ṣ'o ye e?	Is commess you want hear? You don't hear commess yet! You hear?
B'o o ba sọrọ naa fun mi, nwọn o bi daa!	You 'fraid. You can't tangle with me. You born bad/You bastard!
Ọrọ ẹ o jo mi loju! Abi baba repete! Itan ẹ ree lọwọ wa yi!	Your language don't shock nobody. Fat man! Everybody know your business.
Kil'o sọ? O o ri p'ori ẹ o pe!	What you saying? You don't see your head not good?
Ori temi pe daadaa!	My head is quite normal.
Iwọ, tun lu mi k'a woo!	You, you beat me again and you see!

AFRICAN IMPACT ON LITERATURE[10]

Literary Use of Creole

The African legacy of word, idiom, pace, and syntax have predicted that once the artist operates in Creole, African influence is present. Since Creole

is the mother tongue of the majority, oral literature is articulated almost
exclusively either in the basilect or the mesolect. The nationalistic winds of
change in the 1940s gave an impetus to the use of Creole in novelistic and
dramatic dialogue. But Claude McKay (Jamaica) was already a pioneer in
Creole poetry, having since the 1900s written of Jamaican peasant life in
Songs of Jamaica and *Constab Ballads*. His work was an inspiration to Louise
Bennett (Jamaica) who began public performances of her satiric pieces in the
early 1940s. Onomatopeia and reduplication are some of Bennett's tech-
niques which derive from a peasant, and by extension, African, source. Only
Samuel Selvon (Trinidad), however, has dared to write entire novels in the
Creole medium. Timothy Callendar (Barbados) has followed this lead, but in
the short story genre. Vic Reid (Jamaica) used a modified creole in his *New
Day* (1949). Derek Walcott (St. Lucia), playwright and poet, began using
French Creole in his plays from the 1940s, and in his collection of poetry,
Sea Grapes (1976), he used French Creole verse for the first time. Edward
Brathwaite (Barbados) explored the dramatic dialogue potential of Creole
in some of the poems in both *Rights of Passage* (1967), and *Islands* (1969).
The enthusiastic reception of these pieces has inspired younger poets in the
English-speaking Caribbean to use the modified Creole and urban ghetto
language as their poetic medium. The immediacy of the vernacular and
its strong dramatic urgency enhance the message in this form of poetry
which is mainly of a protesting, rebellious, or critical nature.

African Literary Devices in Caribbean Literature

For reasons of ethnocultural continuity, the oral traditions of the English-
speaking Caribbean stem largely from Africa, but it must be stressed that
these traditions share forms, techniques, motifs, and archetypes with the universal imaginative experience of peasant, preliterate peoples. The predominantly African people of the Caribbean absorbed other prevailing cultural
influences during the long period of European colonialism, and their thought
and expression were especially influenced by their metropolitan mother
tongue and, in the English Antilles, the King James version of the Bible. Of lesser
impact were the literary traditions derived from India, China and pre-Colum-
bia America. Since the folklore and literary structures of all these matrices
exhibit common features, these influences have served to reinforce the basic
inherited traditions from Africa. The emphasis on the African impact, therefore, is not intended as an assertion of its exclusivity, but merely for purposes
of an examination of some areas of correspondence between English Carib-

bean verbal expression and that deriving from a major cultural input area across the Atlantic.

Rhythmic Phrasing; Word Music; Word Play

In order to consider some of the techniques that control the use of language in art, it is instructive to analyze the poetic devices evident in this short prayer collected in Trinidad:[11]

Mo njiba alẹ oni	1. I am paying respect to the evening of today.
Alẹ t'o le mi l'oni	2. Evening which covers me today.
Mọ mọ je k'o le mi s'uku	3. Don't let me follow death.
Mọ mọ je k'ole mi s'aran buruku	4. Don't let the thief do me harm.
Mọ mọ jẹ k'o le mi s'elenini	5. Don't let me make a relentless enemy.
Ara t'o nr'oru (= ri oru)	6. The person who uses darkness to his advantage.
Ara t'o nr'okuku (= ri okuku)	7. The person who smells offensively.
Mọ mọ jẹ k'ọn ri mi	8. Don't let him see me.
Mọ nbẹ o si ire l'alẹ yi	9. Here I am. Be beneficent this night.
Baba, o mọ	10. Father, you know.
Jẹ ki mi ji ire l'aurọ	11. Let me wake well in the morning.

We may note the phrasal expansion and repetition of *ale oni* (1) into *ale . . . oni* (2). There is word-play on *le* (2) (cover) and *le* (3, 4, 5) (enable), as well as on *ri* (6) (profit from) and *ri* (7) (be seen/perceived as) and *ri* (8), (see). There are line endings in *-ni, -i, uku*; and there are partial rhymes in *r'oru, r'okuku; si ire, ki ire*. The letter *s* alliterates in lines 3, 4, 5, while phrasal repetition occurs in many lines. The meaning of *s'uku* allows not only the interpretation *sin uku* (accompany death) but also *se uku* (challenge death).

Edward Brathwaite was the first English-speaking Caribbean poet to utilize these devices in patent profusion. Close rhyme brought about by assonance, partial rhyme, and alliteration unifed his poetry in a manner reminiscent of Anglo-Saxon poetry which was itself largely oral and even sung. In fact, these devices are also the hallmark of modern European poetry, thus, illustrating the unconscious reinforcement of submerged traditions by a more obviously accessible one. Brathwaite's poetry had great aural appeal and started established West Indian poetry on a course towards closer identification between poet and people, poetry and folk speech.

> But with the winter I knew
> I was old. Poor
> Tom was cold. Feet
> could no longer walk the fallen
> gold of parks. Gates
> closed, the pavements
> skidded blue and fro-
> zen. To and fro
> I walked, I wandered, wind
> cut my face with its true
> Gillette razor blades and snow
> burnt the rivers' bridges. In my small hired
> room, stretched out upon the New
> York Herald Tribune, pages
> damp from dirty lots, from locked
> out parks, from gutters; dark, tired,
> deaf, cold, too old to care to catch
> alight the quick match of your pity,
> I died alone without the benefit of fire.[12]

Close rhyme and rhythmic pulse are features of verbal skill in Jamaica and these devices are well exploited in its popular music. Below, a young Jamaican poet, Michael Smith, combines these techniques with antiphonic dialogue exchange,[13] interweaving snatches from nursery rhymes. In a lilting delivery, he graphically depicts ugly scenes from Kingston ghetto experience:

> Mi say
> mi kyaa believe it
> Mi say
> mi kyaa believe it.
> Room dem a rent
> mi apply within
> but as mi go in
> cockroach rat and scorpion
> also come in
> Wan' good nose have fe run
> but mi nah go deh
> go sit down pon high wall
> like Hump'y Dump'y.
> Me a face mi reality.
> One little boy come blow him horn

an mi look pon him with scorn
an mi realize mi five boy pickney
was a victim of the trick
dem call partisan politics
An mi ban' mi belly
an mi bawl
an mi ban' mi belly
an mi bawl
an mi ban' mi belly
an mi bawl
Lord!
mi kyaa believe it
mi kyaa believe it
mi say
mi kyaa believe it . . .

Sitting on the curb
with mi friend
talking bout things and time
mi hear one voice say
"Who dat?"
Mi say "A who dat?"
"Who a say 'Who dat?'
when we say 'Who dat?'"
When you take a stock
dem lick we down flat
teeth start fly
an big man start cry
Mi say
mi kyaa believe it
mi say
mi kyaa believe it

In a different mood, Bongo Jerry (Jamaica) uses similar techniques in a classic of poetic prose to lament the death of popular trombonist, Don Drummond:

> Don de Lion
> Blew an iron that was black and blue, a Peter Pan
> to lost black man. A Pied Piper, more music in
> his right hand than Little Boy Blue too . . . .[14]

By juggling sound and meaning, Bongo Jerry places himself firmly in the creative tradition of Rastafarian speech,[15] and utlimately, in a tradition of African poetic art. These tendencies are also evident in the calypso of Trinidad. Commenting on the "see-through" fashion of women's dress, the Mighty Duke had this to sing:

> You could see they bell—ee
> You could see they as (k)—he
> You could see from here—up
> You could see they bus—stop

Verbal Flamboyance—the Boast

The calypso (originally *kaiso*) is a direct descendant of several song types still vigorous in West Africa. There is the moralistic calypso whose contemporary counterpart can be heard in the *apala* music of the Yoruba, to name just one parallel. In this kind of calypso, didacticism of purpose is more important than melodic and rhythmic appeal. This appeal may or may not be present in the other modes of the genre. These include the narrative/humorous/ironic calypso whose point is the display of verbal or situational wit, the calypso which exposes topical scandals, satirizes, or heaps merciless invective on an object of scorn. This last category of calypso necessarily involves the motif of the boast and self-adulation. The singer is brave, fearless, invincible.

> Are you a madman, a fool, or a stranger
> To enter into this source of danger?
> Have you not heard of my quality?
> I am praised in the superlative degree.
> I sat down men on their bended knee
> And teach them not to tamper with me
> For my constitution
> Is made up of an iron barrication,
> San dimanite.[16]

This invective/boast *kaiso* genre is immediately related to the halfchanted utterances of some of the traditional masquerades of Trinidad Carnival. The following are examples of "robber talk."[17] They exhibit the same enchantment with sound and sound symbolism:

> Away down from the vast eyeless regions of the lost
> centuries came I, invincible, undauntable, impregnable . . . .

> My name is Ben Bow. B-EN B-OW stand for Ben Bow. B
> stand for brave deeds that I have done. E, enter into

my dungeon, my goodly man. N, nine days thou shall stay.
B, before you shall be buried, O, O (woe) be unto you
this day. W, when I clash by feet together the earth
crumble, famine follow. Wherever I stand, grass never
grows, sun never shine, far more for mankind to go.
I, Ben Bow, take my right hand and bar the sun and
made it night. I bite off bits of the moon to lengthen
the days and shorten the season . . . . There's no gun,
dagger made of steel, can make me feel or heal . . .[18]

Comparison of these themes and images with the following extract from
Chinua Achebe's *Arrow of God*[19] needs no further comment:

There is a place, Beyond Knowing, where no man or
spirit ventures unless he holds in his right hand
his kith and in his left hand his kin. But I, Ogalanya,
Evil Dog that Warms His Body through the Head, I
took neither kith nor kin and yet went to this place . . . .
When I got there the first friend I made turned out to
be a wizard. I made another friend and found he was a
leper. I, Ogalanya, who cuts *kpom* and pulls *waa*, I
made friends with a leper from whom even a poisoner
flees.

I returned from my sojourn. Afo passed, Nkwo passed,
Eke passed, Oye passed.[20] Afo came round again. I
listened, but my head did not ache, my belly did not
ache; I did not feel dizzy.

Tell me, folk assembled, a man who did this, is his
arm strong or not?

This is the language of confrontation and confrontation had its strongest
cultural outlet in nineteenth and early twentieth century Trinidad in the
kalinda or *bois bataille*—stick fight. Stick-fighting bands were each accompanied by their chantwell (*chanterelle*) or cheerleader who hurled defiance at
his patron's opponents. We may compare the theme, motifs and verbal
formulae of a sample of *kalinda* songs with a Yoruba *ijala* or hunter's songs
Number (3):

1. La vie mwe insho	My life is insured.
La vie mwe insho, salmana	My life is insured, salmana.
La vie mwe insho, salmana	My life is insured, salmana.
Lendi, mardi[21]	Monday, Tuesday.
Mwe ba tini raison	I don't give a damn.

2. Mama, mama	Mama, Mama.
Si tu 'tend ma mort	If you hear of my death.
Pas helez	Don't scream.
Si tu 'tend ma mort	If you hear of my death.
Pas pleurez	Don't cry.
3. Ẹ gb'ohum ẹnu mi ẹgbẹ 'mọ'dẹ,	Listen to my voice, members of the hunters' fraternity.
Mo nre igbo ọdaju o	I am going to the forest, it is certain.
Enia t'o ní iya o pada lẹhin mi	The person who has a mother should not follow me.
Eni o ba ní baba ni o maa kalọ	The one without a father should come, let's go.
Ọdẹ nre igbo ọdaju o . . .	The hunter is going into the forest, that's certain . . . .
Emi nikan ni igbo onigbo o,	I alone in the forest of others.
Emi nikan ni mbe ní jù ọlọ̀tẹ	I alone in the prairie of traitors.
Emi nikan nibiti efon gbe njà ta'ko ta'bo	I alone in the place where both the male and female leopards fight.
Ogbogbó akùgbórí ọmọ a-kù-má-rọ̀[22]	The brave one, the son of the one who does not wither in death.

In Jamaica, contemporary popular music sometimes speaks threateningly of confrontation, but apart from the "rude boy"[23] phase of the late 1960s, confrontation is not posited as much in an individualistic or anecdotal context, as in Trinidad, but rather in communal, generalized terms. The difference stems from obvious social pressures in Jamaica as opposed to the so far buoyant irreverence and cheerful cynicism of the Trinidad personality. Social and economic pressures in Jamaica have found an outlet in a strong messianic hope, epitomized in Rastafarian belief. Because of the dominant Rasta influence on pop music, confrontation and resolution take on visionary and apocalyptic dimensions, dwarfing the limited physical dimensions of the conflict situation posed in Trinidadian *kalinda* and *kaiso* and their African antecedents. In addition, Jamaica's strong *dinky* (dirge) resources have provided a congenial rhythm and cadence for Jamaica's popular music. That music, starting with the forerunners of the *ska* in the late 1950s, was increasingly identified with the lament of the dispossessed. With quickened pace, this music can express happiness and the risqué, but its dominant mood of lament and complaint are conveyed by the monotone tendencies and mournful cadences of its melodic line.

Proverbs

Among other spoken oral literary forms are the proverb, animal tales, tales of the supernatural, historical legends, and creation myths. Jamaica, with a topography that allows far-flung relatively isolated settlements, has retained more proverbs in its basilect and mesolect than has Trinidad. Proverbs are the distillation of the wisdom peasants glean through alert observation of their environment. They may also encapsulate a narrative. Rather than the inability of folk speech to express abstraction, the concrete references reflect the peasant's closeness to nature. Both the kernel and expanded narrative reflect this communal imperative. This language form is therefore sensuous and "alive." That Caribbean literature makes little use of proverbial language is an indication of the distance of the Caribbean writer from the society's peasant base. Barbadian George Lamming's *In the Castle of My Skin* (1953) is definitely enlivened by several proverbial utterances, of African secular and biblical origin.

The Saga

Despite Lamming's highly structured prose, two of his novels utilize the historical legend. In *Of Age and Innocence* (1958), the Tribe Boys recall the indomitable courage and love of liberty displayed by their antecedents in the land—the Amerindians: confronted with subjugation by the conquering Spaniards, they hurled themselves *en masse* over the rocky sea-cliffs and into the Caribbean Sea. This heroic narrative is retold by the younger generation at the time of the island's struggle to obtain independence from colonial rule. It therefore serves as an ethical beacon guiding the actions and attitudes of the island's future leaders. This story is retold in verse by Derek Walcott in *Another Life* (1973). Previously, in his first novel, *Castle of My Skin*, Lamming had told another saga: this time, a village elder recalls the tribe's settled way of life in Africa, the destruction of tribal cohesion with the advent of a cash economy, and the dispersal of the black peoples by the slave trade. Apart from the tribal epic in prose, *Castle of My Skin* also features several personal histories. The lengthy life histories of Bots, Bambi and others are the narrative means used by folk speech to point to social manners, the communal or individual ethos, and the tensions within a society. Walcott uses the same device in some of his early sketches in "Tales of the Islands" (1948-60), and expands the technique in *Another Life* to such dimensions and with such resonance that certain characters, particularly Anna, St. Omer, and Simmonds take on mythological significance.

Allegory: The Dream Vision

The allegorical narrative has made only limited impact on written Caribbean literature. Yet the folk imagination still works and expresses itself strongly in terms of symbols that are largely apprehended in dreams and visions. In his play, *Dream on Monkey Mountain* (1967), Derek Walcott uses the elaborate fantasy of a dream to explore the tortured and ambivalent attitudes toward color and ethnicity in Caribbean society. And in his novels, Wilson Harris (Guyana) often makes use of revelation by dream to arouse the consciousness of his "characters."

The following extract from a conversation with a Kumina Queen[24] in Jamaica is not an account of a dream, but indicates a symbolically charged perception of real personal experience:

> One day, I remember one day I find some lilies and I plant the
> lilies them in row, and one Sunday morning when I wake all the
> lilies blow. Seven lilies and is seven of them blow. And I
> leave and go down in the gully bottom to go and pick up some
> coconut and when I go I see a cotton tree and I just fell
> right down at the cotton tree root. And is there I take now.
> Well, I don't eat anything. Twenty one days and I don't eat.
> In the nights in the cotton tree coming like it hollow and
> I inside there. And you have some grave around that cotton
> tree, right round it some tombs, but those is some old-time
> Africans, you understand? Well, those tombs around the cotton
> tree and I inside of the cotton tree lay down and at nighttime
> I see the cotton tree light up with candles and I resting now
> put my hand this way sleeping and I only hear a little voice
> come to me and them talking to me but those things is spirit
> talking to me and them speaking to me now . . . .

In West Indian fiction, Harris's novels are closest to this symbolist quality of perception. Inspired originally by Amerindian lore, Harris's ontology draws heavily on archetypes and motifs of universal mythology; it thus shares the perspective of nontechnological societies where the parameters of vision and reality are not discrete. This accounts for the convergence of linear moments in time and the identity of persons and objects as pivotal techniques with

Harris. These techniques are shared with the Latin American literary genre of "magical realism." The extent of the convergence in the folk imagination of empirically discrete objects can be judged from this account of a Trinidadian stick-fight:[25]

> Once I was playing with a fellow right here by the name
> of Altenar. As soon as Altenar carré (squared up with
> the stick) like that so, I notice a big door in front of
> him. I call a fellow name Maitland. I say "Buddy Maitland,
> watch that man." He say "Buddy, me see long time." He
> (Altenar) have a door and he behind the door stooping down,
> but you seeing a man in front of you with a stick, but he is
> behind the door. As soon as he move that door you see a big
> tree come, and the tree, as soon as he raise his hand, all
> the branches is coming down on you, you have to run. So
> Maitland tell me "Buddy, lef him to me." And Maitland
> just watch him and give him a Cross (made the sign of the
> Cross in front of Altenar) and walk up on him and give him
> bow. He (Altenar) gone do lai do, do lai do, and shortly
> after he die.

Allegory is a favorite device of the kaiso also, particularly, though not exclusively, when delicacy of presentation is required. The kaiso audience may reject an overtly lewd calypso, but it is absolutely fascinated by a calypso expressed in double entendre. Here, Small Island Pride describes a romantic rendezvous. He has been hired as the "driver" of a "Ford motor car:"

> Well, after examination
> We went out on demonstration
> She drive ten miles and a quarter
> I told her "Stop, turn the wheel over"
> Well, when I start me fast driving
> Lots of funny things start happening
> The wire cross on another
> The water hose burst loose the radiator
> Well, the gear-box started a grinding
> This gear so hard I can't get it go in
> So I pull out me gear-lever
> Water fly through the muffler
> And the whole car went on fire.

The allegorical tradition is reclaimed by Dennis Scott (Jamaica) in his unforgettable poem Uncle Time (1950s). It has also been coopted into the drama of the region. *Dance Bongo* (1965) by Errol Hill (Trinidad) portrays Fate or Death in the person of the stick-fighter/ stranger and weaves a tale of retribution around village customs. Derek Walcott's *Ti Jean* (1958) is significant for its use of several folkloric devices: the storyteller, the *conte*, animal characters, characters with multiple identity, triplication motifs in character and incident, and the enactment of a parable on human attitudes, social evolution, and the blessedness of life itself. Like *Dance Bongo, Ti Jean* incorporates mime, masque, music and dance with poetry. In both, the music draws in varying degrees on the Trinidad stick fight, calypso, and wake traditions. Younger students of drama like Rawle Gibbon (Trinidad), Al Creighton, and Honor Ford-Smith (Jamaica) are currently exploring the theatrical elements to be found in the symbolic shape, gesture, and language of religious and secular rituals of the largely African-derived folk.[26]

Folk Narrative

The conditions for the survival of a vital folktale tradition, however, are fading fast. In Trinidad, Compé Lapin (Brer Rabbit) and his band of animal victims disappeared with the decline of the French Creole language in the early part of the twentieth century: they are now being introduced to children via the written medium. In Jamaica the Akan Anansi is alive as a symbol of *samfie*—conmanship—but the eagerness of university students to research the traditions of Anansi, the spider, is at marked variance with the reality that most of them, whether from the town or country, have never had Anansi stories narrated to them in childhood. On the other hand, the storytelling art has recently been revived by Paul Keans-Douglas (Grenada), and "Shake" Keane (St. Vincent).[27] Louis Bennett has long been an exponent of the Anansi story on record and radio and through theatrical performance. Samuel Selvon, meanwhile, has adapted in several of his novels the "old-talk," or ballad narrative form heard minutely in Trinidad.

The transformations and multiple personalities of Anansi have provided recent Caribbean literature with a fertile symbol and technical focus. "Shake" Keane, Edward Brathwaite, and both Andrew Salkey[28] and Sylvia Wynter (Jamaica) are among those who have utilized this fascinating resource. In *Islands* Brathwaite explores Anansi as a half-forgotten symbol of the African-Caribbean link. In her pantomine *Rockstone Anancy* (1970), Wynter seeks to integrate the "trickster aspect" of the spiderman with "his Creator-god-hero aspect."[29]

Folkloric motifs of incident, item, and structure are, however, almost entirely absent from Caribbean scribal literature. One exception is *Ti Jean*, already mentioned. Another interesting departure is found in *The Last Enchantment* (1960) where Neville Dawes (Jamaica) does not modify the folktale genre as Walcott does in his play, but rather ends his narrative with a complete tale culled from the oral tradition. Significantly, the I-narrator extols it as "the perfect story no writer could ever write." The repetition and interlocking cumulative structure, called *aro* in Yoruba, lends interest, rhythm, and symmetry to the piece. On the surface, it might appear that its tight, condensed structure does not lend itself to novelistic expansion, but here is a challenge for the creative artist.

> Once when Anancy was a little boy he going on an' him
> see Ping-Wing bramble wid a rat. Him fight Ping-Wing
> take 'way the rat so carry it hang it up in the kitchen.
> When him was gawn Granny came een an' eat off the rat.
> When Anancy come back him cyan fine the rat. Him say,
> 'Come, come Granny give me me rat, me rat come from Ping-
> Wing, Ping-Wing juk me han', me han' come from God' . . . .

CONCLUSION

Describing the impact of colonization on literary output, Sylvia Wynter has written: "When . . . an invading civilization decapitates the learned tradition of another culture and replaces it, then a disjuncture occurs between the 'little' tradition and the 'high' tradition. Where one is written and the other oral, the disjuncture is even greater. The lack of any real creative literature in a colonial society comes from the fact that the literate are educated to despise the 'oral' tradition of the people and to see the written tradition as the only vehicle for culture. The high tradition suffers from inanition, a lack of roots to feed on; the little tradition is alive and vigorous but suffers from the lack of a learned tradition to interact with."[30]

Pioneer Caribbean writing of the 1930s and 1940s was strongly influenced by the narrative techniques of the Victorians, the rhythms of Carlyle, the phraseology of the Augustan and Romantic schools. As a literature whose authors are generally travelled and erudite, the *literati* of the society, a variety of international influences are quite understandably perceived in this body of work: Shakespeare, Donne, Hemingway, Eliot, the Absurdists, Joyce, Auden, Richard Wright.

At the same time, however, political trends have, from the early decades of the century, been pressuring the Caribbean *literati* to pay closer attention to the masses—both their social and political experience and their artistic expression.

In terms of content the theme of Africa has been prominent in Caribbean writing. This, as a by-product of the agonized issue of ethnic and cultural loyalties. To heighten the conflict and choice, some writers have set Caribbean man in Africa itself: from Guyana Denis Williams, *Other Leopards* (1963), and O. R. Dathorne, *The Scholar Man* (1964); Walcott, *Dream on Monkey Mountain* (1967); Brathwaite, *Masks* (1968). In *The Leopard* (1958), Vic Reid located his mulatto—symbol of West Indian culture—in colonial Mau-Mau Kenya. Thus, the theme of Africa has been more obvious than the technical legacy which both folk and learned artist in the Caribbean have derived from Africa.[31] So far, only Brathwaite's *Masks* has consciously aimed at and achieved the quality and structure of African traditional court poetry, praise song, incantation, and dirge. So much so that the Ghanian dramatist, Ana Ata Aidoo, was moved to call it "naked Akan."[32] Perhaps, acquaintance with traditional and modern African literature will further revitalize the literate traditions of Caribbean writing and alert the "high" tradition to the African literary retentions in peasant speech and song. Study of African languages is another means by which we can become attuned to the African influences of Caribbean Creole languages as well as to indigenous literary expression.

Literary forms are reflections of modes of social organization, the ethos, the technological level and pace of a community. It would be unrealistic therefore to expect that a new society would retain unchanged old modes of expression. Several factors have deprived many oral literary modes of their viability in modern society—factors such as the erosion of the communal peasant life-style, urban and rural electrification, the spread of the visual mass media in particular, the expansion of professional and leisure activities, together with increasing reliance on empirical thought.[33] At the same time, the society and its writers are becoming increasingly aware of this inherited resource for literary and language models. They will no doubt soon reclaim the metaphoric wealth, the legend, history, and structural organization of the African songs and poetry that are being unearthed in the Caribbean itself. Just as the Creoles are the result of the creative fusion of several linguistic parents, so too, one anticipates an adaptation of traditional literary modes, under the impetus of continuing political and cultural imperatives.

Already, in fact, African gods are reinforcing written Caribbean literature as symbols of tradition, courage, subversion, and revolt,[34] with both Brathwaite and Harris calling attention to the symbolism of the lame African deity whose role is, ironically, guardian of the gate or pathway, and therefore guide and liberator.[35] But in modern Jamaican popular music and poetry, the most formidable god of redemption is Jah, the apotheosis in

Rastafarian belief of Ethiopia's former emperor, Haile Selassie. Another such symbol is the Jamaican pan-Africanist, Marcus Garvey, whose sayings, both real and mythical, have long been and are increasingly being given prophetic significance.[36] To add to all this, the revolutionary political atmosphere of Jamaica during the 1970s has caused the anticolonial and antiimperialist struggles in Mozambique, Angola, Zimbabwe, and South Africa to provide subject-matter for popular songs, and in recent poetry to serve as inspirational symbols of the eventual triumph of Caribbean man over oppression.[37]

In whatever form, reclamation of the African cultural and political links are part of a process of psychological freedom from the negative impact of a warping slave and colonial/neocolonial past. In poetic prose, the novelist aptly describes the liberating effects of this reconciliation with past and self:

I was a god again, drunk on the mead of the
land, and massive with the sun chanting in my
veins. And so, flooded with the bright clarity
of my acceptance, I held this lovely wayward
island, starkly, in my arms.[38]

NOTES

1. On African languages in Cuba see David Olmsted, "Comparative Notes on Yoruba and Lucumí," *Language*, 29 (1953): 157-64; Fabelo Díaz, "Lengua de santeros" *Guiné Gongorí*, (1956); Lydia Cabrera, *Anagó, Vocabulario Lucumí* (Havana, 1957); Pedro Deschamps Chapeaux, "El Lenguaje Abakuá" *Etnología y Folklore* 4 (1967): 39-48.

2. David Dalby, "Ashanti Survivals in the Language and Traditions of the Windward Maroons of Jamaica," *African Language Studies* 12 (1971): 31-51.

3. Recent studies on the subject of African indentured labor into the West Indies include: J. Asiegbu, *Slavery and the Politics of Liberation, 1787-1861: A Study of Liberated African Emigration and British Anti-Slavery Policy* (London, 1970); M. E. Thomas, *Jamaica and Voluntary Laborers from Africa, 1840-1865* (Florida, 1974); Monica Schuler, " 'Yerri, Yerri, Koongo': A Social History of Liberated African Immigration into Jamaica, 1841-1867," (Ph.D. diss., University of Wisconsin, 1977).

4. Trinidad's population consists of East Indians and Africans, with a minority of Chinese, Lebanese, and Europeans of British, French, Spanish, and Portuguese origin.

5. This deterioration is particularly noticeable among those who have not learned Yoruba directly from their parents or grandparents.

6. This feature of syntactic simplification may be cited as an instance of language universals in operation. As a feature of Creole languages, this tendency must also have received reinforcement from French and English creoles.

7. To my knowledge, collection of this material has been done only by Dr. J. D. Elder and myself.

8. Some contributions on the issue are: Robert Hall, Jr., "Creolized Languages and 'Genetic Relationships,' " *Word* 14 (1958): 367-73; Robert Thompson, "A Note

on Some Possible Affinities Between the Creole Dialects of the Old World and Those of the New," *Creole Language Studies* 2 (1961): 107-13; Douglas Taylor, "The Origin of West Indian Creole Languages—Evidence from Grammatical Categories," *American Anthropologist* 65 (1963): 800-814; Mervyn Alleyne, "The Linguistic Continuity of Africa in the Caribbean," *Black Academy Review* 1, no. 4 (Winter 1970): 3-16; Ian Hancock, "A Provisional Comparison of the English-based Atlantic Creoles," in *Pidginization and Creolization of Languages*, ed. Dell Hymes, (New York, 1971); David Ola Oke, "On the Genesis of New World Black English," *Caribbean Quarterly* 23, no. 1 (March 1977): 61-79. David DeCamp gives a survey of the evolution of and controversial issues involved in creole language studies in "The Development of Pidgin and Creole Studies," in *Symposium on Cultural Identity of French-Speaking in the Americas*, ed. Albert Valdman, (Bloomington, 1977), pp. 3-20.

9. A few such contributions are: Jean D'Costa and Jack Berry, "Some Considerations of Tone in Jamaican Creole"; David Lawton, "Tone and Jamaican Creole"; Raymond Relouzat, "Structure Comparée de la Phrase Ewe et de la Phrase Créole"—all papers presented to the Conference on Caribbean Linguistics, Jamaica, 1971; Frank Cassidy, "Jamaican Creole and Twi—Some Comparisons," *Conference on Creole Languages and Educational Development* (Trinidad, 1972); Richard Price, "Kikoongo and Saramaccan: a Reappraisal," *Journal of African Languages* 12 (1973) George Huttar, "Some Kwalike Features of Djuka Syntax," Summer Institute of Linguistics, (Australia, 1974).

10. Helpful suggestions in regard to this section of the paper came from discussions at the Caribbean Literature Seminar, University of the West Indies, Mona, Jamaica, 9 December 1977.

11. Sandrin LeGendre, Marabella.

12. *Rights of Passage*, "Didn't He Ramble."

13. This is a dominant technique in the Creole poetry of Bruce St. John (Barbados) and Trevor Rhone (Jamaica).

14. *Abeng*, 17 May 1969.

15. Sound symbolism is very important in Rasta speech, in addition to which words are reconstructed to make sememes indicate positive/negative attributes. Thus "I-man" (I) to stress the humanity of each human being, "I" being symbolic of the eye, the visionary potential, and of the God in man. "Overstand" (understand) indicates grasp and dominion over phenomena; "U-blind" (UC, i.e., University College) conveys the poison of the white man's education. Characteristically, a Rasta, recently questioned on his diet, replied that he was only concerned with "liveth."

16. "Without pity."

17. The robber masquerade wears a broad, round-brimmed, fringed hat with a high peaked crown. Such hats are worn by chiefs in the rivers area of Southeastern Nigeria. These hats were imported into the West African coastal areas from Europe. See also P.C. Lloyd, ed., "Osifekunde of Ijebu", ed. Philip Curtin, *Africa Remembered*, (Madison, Wis., 1967), p. 264, n. 125.

18. In Daniel Crowley, "The Midnight Robbers," *Caribbean Quarterly* 4, nos. 3 and 4 (1956):268.

19. Heinemann, 1970 reprint, p. 48.

20. Days of the week.

21. The days of Carnival, immediately preceding Ash Wednesday.

22. "Ijuba Ode" in Oladipo Yemitan, ed., *Ijala-Are Ode* (Nigeria, 1963), p. 50. Acknowledgments of assistance in translation are due to Dr. Simi Afonja and Mr. Funso Aiyejina, both of the University of Ife, Nigeria. Further comparisons can be made with this war chant, which was used by Haitian blacks whenever on the attack in the revolution:

Grenadier a laso	Grenadiers to the assault.
Sa ki mouri zafe a yo	What is death?
Nan pouin manman	We have no mother.
Nan pouin pitit	No child.
Sa ki mouri zafe a yo	What is death?

in Maximilien Laroche, "The myth of the Zombi," in *Exile and Tradition: Studies in African and Caribbean Literature*, ed. Roland Smith (Halifax, Nova Scotia, 1976), pp. 44-61.

23. "Antisocial person, criminal."

24. Imogene Kennedy, Kingston.

25. Albert Pierre, Sumsum Hill, Claxton Bay.

26. Errol Hill, *The Trinidad Carnival—Mandate for a National Theatre* (Austin, Texas, 1972), culminated Hill's long-standing advocacy of the incorporation of elements from the folk theatre into formal drama.

27. Cf. E. McG., "Shake" Keane, "Nancitori," *Bim* 15, no. 57 (March 1974): 57-62; and Paul Keans-Douglas, *When Moon Shine* (London, 1975) available also on record.

28. *Anancy's Score* (1973).

29. Program notes.

30. Paper submitted to Inter-Departmental Seminar on Caribbean Content of Courses at the University of the West Indies, Mona, Jamaica, 15 June 1971.

31. For studies on the thematic relevance of Africa to Caribbean literature, see O. R. Dathorne, "Africa in West Indian Literature," in *Black Orpheus* 16 (1964): 42-54; George Lamming, "Caribbean Literature: The Black Rock of Africa," *African Forum* 1, no. 4 (Spring 1966): 32-52; Arthur Drayton, "West Indian Consciousness in West Indian Verse: A Historical Perspective," *Journal of Commonwealth Literature* 9 (July 1970): 66-88. For studies on the use and influence of African literary techniques, see Samuel Asein, "The Concept of Form—A Study of Some Ancestral Elements in Brathwaite's Trilogy," *African Studies Association of the West Indies Bulletin* 4 (1971): 9-38; Maureen Warner Lewis, "Odomankoma 'Kyerema Se . . .," *Caribbean Quarterly* 19, no. 2 (June 1973): 51-99; Edward Brathwaite, "The African Presence in Caribbean Literature," *Daedalus* 103 (Spring 1974), pp. 73-109; Olabiyi Yai, "Influence Yoruba dans la poésie Cubaine: Nicolás Guillén et la tradition poétique Yoruba" (Seminar Paper, Department of Modern European Languages, University of Ife, Nigeria, 1975).

32. Ana Ata Aidoo, "Akan and English," *West Africa* (21 September 1968), p. 1099.

33. By the early 1950s, in researching on "Parent-Teacher Relationships in a Jamaican Village," Edward Seaga discovered negative parent attitudes to the teaching of Anansi stories in school. "Is only black people tek dem kind of story serious and is why we so idiot." "It only teach dem to lie and t'ief," in *Consequences of Class and Color—West Indian Perspectives*, ed. David Lowenthal and Lambros Comitas (New York, 1975), p. 173.

34. See among others, Claude McKay, *Banana Bottom* (New York, 1933), George Lamming, *Season of Adventure* (London, 1960), Sylvia Wynter, *Hills of Hebron* (New York, 1962), Edward Brathwaite, *Islands* (New York, 1969).

35. See Wilson Harris, *Tradition, the Writer and Society* (London, 1967), 50-52; Edward Brathwaite, "Legba," *Island* (New York, 1969).

36. See songs by Burning Spear and "Seven Miles of Black Star Liners" by Fred Locks.

37. See songs by Bob Marley and Pablo Moses; poems by Michael Smith, by Orlando Wong in *Echo* (1977), Edward Brathwaite, "Soweto" (1976), and Brian Meeks, "Next Stop—Johannesburg" (1976).

38. Neville Dawes, *The Last Enchantment* (London, 1960).

THE AFRICAN PRESENCE
IN THE POETRY OF NICOLÁS GUILLÉN

Lorna V. Williams

For most blacks living in the Americas, Africa is the continent from which one's ancestors came, but it is hardly the place where one seeks poetic inspiration in the present. Time and space remain frozen in that mythical primeval moment, when one's ancestors were forced to embark on the slave ships traveling to the New World. Since few residents of the Americas have a first-hand knowledge of the land of their forefathers, popular fantasies of Africa form a standard part of the collective memory of black peoples in the New World. The presence that once was Africa has been displaced by Europe, as the languages spoken in the Americas so eloquently attest. And yet, centuries of miscegenation have failed to eliminate all trace of Africa from the socio-cultural repertoire of blacks in the New World. Or rather, the awareness that one is no longer as one's ancestors were has often led blacks to assert their continuity with an ideal African past, which predates contact with the "corrupting" influences of Euro-American civilization.

In this respect, the poetry of the Afro-Cuban, Nicolás Guillén, is instructive. In the opening lines of the *Son número 6* (*Son number 6*), Guillén declares himself to be Yoruba. However, by the middle of the second stanza, it becomes evident that the persona is no longer the representative of a particular ethnic group, but rather the spokesman for what M. G. Smith would term a generalized African culture[1]

Yoruba soy,
cantando voy,

llorando estoy,
y cuando no soy yoruba,
soy congo, mandinga, carabalí.

[I am Yoruba
singing along,
weeping,
and when I am not Yoruba,
I am Kongo, Mandinka, Calabar.]
(I:231)[2]

The poem thereafter becomes a celebration of that cultural convergence, which has often been regarded as a characteristic of black societies in the New World. If on the existential plane, ethnic identity becomes interchangeable, in rhetorical terms, the primacy of Yoruba culture is upheld through the force of repetition, thereby reflecting the cultural reality of Cuba.[3]

Frequent references to Shango, and mention of his wife, Oshun, whose protection is invoked even for Stalin, also serve to highlight the predominance of the Yoruba influence in Cuba. Since it is generally acknowledged that the religious domain has remained the most faithful reflection of the African presence in the New World, it is possible to regard the red beads worn by the black woman who dances through the pages of *Sóngoro cosongo* as a sign that she is a worshipper of Shango, and to note that one of his sacrificial foods, *quimbombó* (okra stew), has become part of the national diet, which the nostalgic tourist dreams of in Paris.[4] As the *Balada del güije* (*Ballad of the River Spirit*) makes clear, being a worshipper of Shango, or even wearing his insignia, does not offer unlimited protection against death or misfortune. It would appear that in this case, the necklace has lost its mystical power, and should have been specially treated by the priest so as to endow it with the miraculous power of the god that would have saved the child's life.[5]

It should be noted that the cause of death is not found in the malfunctioning of the child's body, or even in an accident. Instead, intentionality is attributed to the river, which is peopled with beings that devour black children and other passers-by. In granting the river a spiritual dimension, Guillén reveals his characters to be living in an anthropomorphic universe, as did the members of traditional African societies.[6] Since meaning is perceived in the objects of the natural world, which are often the dwelling place of a divinity, man is obliged to propitiate them to maintain harmony in the universe. In this case, words are used as incantation, as the mother hopes to dispel misfortune by repeating:

¡Ñeque, que se vaya el ñeque!
¡Güije, que se vaya el güije!

[Curse, may the curse go away!
River-spirit, may the river-spirit go away!]
(I:143-45)

Here the word, which ordinarily is believed to have the capacity to ward off disaster, by virtue of its symbolical role as a means of transmitting divine power, has ceased to be effective, as it too seems to have lost its mystical force.[7]

That the word may possess this mystical power is amply demonstrated by *Sensemayá*, the "chant for killing a snake." In this instance, the word is charged with sufficient spiritual force as to produce the desired effect. Undoubtedly, the results of the chant are dependent on the manner in which it is uttered. In Guillén's hands, verbal expression attains the condition of music, as the author exploits the percussive possibilities in the name of one of the Kongo peoples to set the basic rhythm of the poem:

¡Mayombe—bombe—mayombé!
¡Mayombe—bombe—mayombé!
¡Mayombe—bombe—mayombé!
(I:147-49)

While the octosyllabic meter of the choral repetitions serves as the frame of reference for the entire performance, the call-and-response structure of the poem makes polymeter possible, for verses of contrasting meters are used to mark the states of the snake's progress. A syncopated rhythm is also achieved through the manipulation of a limited vocabulary, which depends for its effectiveness on the recurrence of set phrases with contrasting patterns of accentuation. This becomes most pronounced in the final stanza, where the heterophonic mode of the choral response marks the death of Sensemayá:

¡Mayombe—bomebe—mayombé!
Sensemayá, la culebra . . .
¡Mayombe—bombe—mayombé!
Sensemayá, no se mueve . . .
¡Mayombe—bombe—mayombé!
Sensemayá, la culebra . . .
¡Mayombe—bombe—mayombé!
Sensemayá, see murió.

[Mayombe—bombe—mayombe!
Sensemayá, the serpent . . .

Mayombe—bombe—mayombé!
Sensemayá, is not moving . . .
Mayombe—bombe—mayombé!
Sensemayá, the serpent . . .
Mayombe—bombe—mayombé!
Sensemayá, it is dead.]

(I:148-49)

The oral quality of the poem reveals its grounding in an African conception of the role of the human voice, which in musical composition is the primary instrument around which all others converge.[8]

However, as Ruth Finnegan indicates, in verbal compositions which are sung, sound often takes precedence over sense, as the rhythmic requirements of the music make the use of nonsense words and onomatopoeia necessary.[9] Guillén's preference for the *jitanjáfora* in his early poetry is therefore in keeping with this widespread tendency of the African lyric. At the same time, it should be pointed out that whereas the lyric is only one of the many genres in African literature, and that while one of its characteristic features results from the subordination of meaning to melody, for many New World writers of Guillén's generation, the lyrical divorce between sound and sense comes to symbolize the nature of African man.

As G. R. Coulthard has observed, the Spenglerian atmosphere prevailing in Europe in the decade after the First World War was conducive to the adoption of such a stance, since many people who were disillusioned with European intellectual endeavor as manifested in its death-dealing technology, were searching for an Adamic world in which being was no longer inhibited by thought.[10] Since Africa had always been perceived to lie on the periphery of Europe, which was the center from which all visions of culture were projected, it readily came to occupy that ideal space as a continent in which man lives in a state of nature, unencumbered by the processes of rational thought. To Caribbean writers who generally took their cue from Europe, and for whom Africa was equally out of focus, despite the fact that they were surrounded by living reminders of the African connection, the celebration of African spontaneity became a means of asserting their American vitality and originality in the face of the evident "decline" of Europe. In O. R. Dathorne's terms, ignorance and desire caused this literary vision of Africa to acquire the characteristics of a landscape of the mind,[11] since it was required to be everything that Europe was not.

Many prevailing attitudes toward Africa are present in Guillén's early work. For example, the causes of the migration to the Americas are not sought in the internal structure of particular African societies, which would explain how many slaves arrived in the New World as a result of political expediency, socioeconomic necessity, or even human ruthlessness and greed, as recent scholarly research has since demonstrated.[12] Instead, as the *Balada de los dos abuelos* (*Ballad of the Two Grandfathers*) indicates, the African is portrayed as an innocent victim of superior European cunning, easily tempted by a few worthless beads into the holds of the slave ship. The pilgrimage to the Americas begins at an unlocalized point in space, where man has not yet imposed his imprint on the landscape. The hot, humid jungles teeming with monkeys and alligators therefore appear as a metonymic sign for a continent, whose most distinguishing feature is its primitiveness:

Africa de selvas húmedas
y de gordos gongos sordos . . .
—¡Me muero!
(Dice mi abuelo negro.)
Aguaprieta de caimanes,
verdes mañanas de cocos . . .
—¡Me canso!
(Dice mi abuelo blanco.)
Oh velas de amargo viento,
galeón ardiendo en oro . . .
—¡Me muero!
(Dice mi abuelo negro.)
¡Oh costas de cuello virgen
engañadas de abalorios . . .!
—¡Me canso!
(Dice mi abuelo blanco.)
¡Oh puro sol repujado,
preso en el aro del trópico;
oh luna redonda y limpia
sobre el sueño de los monos!

[Africa of the humid jungles
and big, muffled drums . . .
—I am dying!
(Says my black grandfather.)
Water blackish with alligators,
mornings green with coconuts . . .
—I am tired!
(Says my white grandfather.)
Oh ships sailing in a bitter wind,
galleon on fire for gold . . .

—I am dying!
(Says my black grandfather.)
Oh coasts of virgin necks
deceived with glass beads . . .!
—I am tired!
(Says my white grandfather.)
Oh pure, embossed sun,
imprisoned in the hoop of the tropics;
Oh moon, round and limpid
above the sleep of monkeys!]
(I:138)

Here man and nature share the same unspoiled condition, as conveyed by the references to "virgin necks," "pure sun," and "limpid moon." Equally significant is the fact that the European grandfather is characterized by his eyes, the principal organ of perception, while the African grandfather is presented as an earthy, muscular creature:

Pie desnudo, torso pétreo
los de mi negro;
pupilas de vidrio antártico
las de mi blanco.

[Bare foot, stony torso
those of my black one;
pupils of antarctic glass
those of my white one.]
(I:137)

Implicit in the vision of elemental strength embodied by the prototypical African ancestor is the idea of mindless energy, totally committed to a life of sensuality. In this connection, *Madrigal* comes readily to mind. To a certain extent, the poem can be regarded as merely a *machista* portrayal of the black woman:

Tu vientre sabe más que tu cabeza
y tanto como tus muslos.
Esa
es la fuerte gracia negra
de tu cuerpo desnudo.

Signo de selva el tuyo,
con tus collares rojos,
tus brazaletes de oro curvo,

y ese caimán oscuro
nadando en el Zambeze de tus ojos.

[Your belly knows more than your head
and as much as your thighs.
That
is the strong black charm
of your naked body.

Yours is the mark of the jungle,
with your red necklaces,
your bracelets of curved gold,
and that dark alligator
swimming in the Zambezi of your eyes.]
                    (I:121-22)

However, her metaphorical attributes reveal that her sensuality is an atavistic quality, transmitted to her by her African forebears.

The aconceptual propensity of the African explains his willingness to indulge in singing and dancing, preferably to the pulsating rhythms of the drum. Add alcoholic stupor, and we have the major ingredients of the then popular image of African man:

¡Yambambó, yambambé!
Repica el congo solongo,
repica el negro bien negro;
congo solongo del Songo
baila yambó sobre un pie.

Mamatomba,
serembe cuserembá.

El negro canta y se ajuma,
el negro se ajuma y canta,
el negro canta y se va.

Acuememe serembó,
              aé,
          yambó,
              aé.

Tamba, tamba, tamba, tamba,
tamba del negro que tumba;
tumba del negro, caramba,
caramba, que el negro tumba:
¡yamba, yambó, yambambé!

[Yambambó, yambambé!
The Kongo solongo is ringing,
the black man, the real black man, is ringing;
the Kongo solongo from the Songo
is dancing the yambó on one foot.

Mamatomba,
serembe cuserembá.
The black man sings and gets drunk,
the black man gets drunk and sings,
the black man sings and goes away.

Acuememe serembó,
      aé,
    yambó,
      aé,

Bam, bam, bam, bam,
bam of the black man who tumbles;
drum of the black man, wow,
wow, oh the black man is tumbling:
yamba, yambó, yambambé!]
          (I:122-23)

Canto negro (*Black Song)* is no doubt one of the poems which Lloyd King has in mind when he states that Afro-Cubanism simply perpetuates the stereotypical image of the black man as primitive.[13] Indeed, the very form of the poem is the expression of its referential dimension, for it defies translation because its semantic content is at such a minimum. It therefore establishes that the pleasure-seeking creature, which is its subject, has a limited capacity to articulate meaningful sounds.

And yet, perhaps the isolated fragments of intelligible sound—"congo," "Songo," "yambó"—correspond to what Edward Brathwaite would perceive as a genuine desire to reestablish the link with Africa,[14] particularly since, according to Fernando Ortiz, there was still a significant number of the population who had been born in Africa living in Cuba at the time when Guillén came of age.[15] However, as George Lamming has indicated, for the Caribbean writer who lives in a culture where the dominant values are European oriented, the attempt at reconnection is a problematic enterprise, because Africa is so carefully screened from his consciously lived experience. The result is often a feeling of ambivalence.[16] Guillén's poem, ironically entitled *Mujer nueva* (*New Woman*), serves as an example of this ambivalent attitude, for in his enumeration of the positive qualities of this new African woman, he reduces her to an animal-like status by referring to her *anca fuerte* (strong haunch) (I: 120).

Undoubtedly, as Lamming has asserted, the dilemma of the Afro-Caribbean writer stems from the fact that while he recognizes Africa's contribution to the shaping of his own being, for him, Africa as historical and geographical entity has ceased to have tangible existence.[17] Consequently, as in Guillén's poem, *La canción del bongó* (*Song of the bongo*), the name, "Bondó," comes to represent absolute negativity:

> *siempre falta* algún abuelo
> cuando no sobra algún Don
> y hay títulos de Castilla
> con parientes en Bondó:
>
> [some grandfather *is always missing*,
> when some Sir is not left over
> and there are titles from Castile
> with relatives in Bondó:]
>   (I:117)[18]

Since the negation of Africa also implies the negation of part of his being, the Caribbean writer often attempts to fill the void with "human significance."[19] But this attempt can only be partially successful, for in his engagement with that continent, the writer soon recognizes that he has lost the key to deciphering its true meaning. Names, places, people, kinship systems, political affiliation, nationality—in fact, all the relationships that serve to anchor the self in a society—have now passed into a state of otherness. Hence the sense of loss, so admirably expressed in Guillén's *El apellido* (*The Family Name*). The crossing of the Atlantic had led to a severing of the links with those who stayed behind: which explains the vaporous nature of the imagery, each time an effort is made to recall the point of origin:

> ¿Ya conocéis mi sangre navegable,
> mi geografía llena de oscuros montes,
> de hondos y amargos valles
> que no están en los mapas?
> ¿Acaso visitasteis mis abismos,
> mis galerías subterráneas
> con grandes piedras húmedas,
> islas sobresaliendo en negras charcas
> y donde un puro chorro
> siento de antiguas aguas

caer desde mi alto corazón
con fresco y hondo estrépito
en un lugar lleno de ardientes árboles,
monos equilibristas,
loros legisladores y culebras?

[Do you already know my navigable blood,
my geography full of dark mountains,
of deep and bitter valleys
that are not on the maps?
Did you by chance visit by abysses,
my underground galleries
with big, damp stones,
islands jutting out from black pools
and where I feel a pure stream
of ancient waters
fall from my high heart
with a fresh and deep crash
into a place full of burning trees,
acrobatic monkeys,
legislating parrots and snakes?]
                    (I:395)

No doubt because the new environment does not offer enough scope for
self-actualization, there is a stubborn insistence on inscribing oneself in the
original frame of reference:

¿Seré Yelofe?
¿Nicolás Yelofe, acaso?
¿O Nicolás Bakongo?
¿Tal vez Guillén Banguila?
¿O Kumbá?
¿Quizá Guillén Kumbá?
¿O Kongué?
¿Pudiera ser Guillén Kongué?

[Am I Yelofe?
Nicolás Yelofe perhaps?
Or Nicolás Bakongo?
Perchance Guillén Banguila?
Or Kumbá?
Maybe Guillén Kumbá?

Or Kongué?
Could I be Guillén Kongué?]
(I:397)

However, the series of rhetorical questions point to the bewildering nature of such an undertaking. While the family names selected are indeed authentic, they represent groups widely separated on the continent, and so pose the problem of belonging, or rather no longer belonging, even more acutely.

The anguished search for roots has been created by a breakdown in the system of communication:

¿No tengo pues
un abuelo mandinga, congo, dahomeyano?
¿Cómo se llama? ¡Oh, sí, decídmelo!
¿Andrés? ¿Francisco? ¿Amable?
¿Cómo decís Andrés en congo?
¿Cómo habéis dicho siempre
Francisco en dahomeyano?
En mandinga ¿cómo se dice Amable?

[Don't I then have
a Mandinka, Congolese, Dahomean grandfather?
What is his name? On, yes, tell it to me!
Andrés? Francisco? Amable?
How do you say Andrés in Congolese?
How have you always said
Francisco in Dahomean?
In Mandinka, how do you say Amable?]
(I:396)

By no longer speaking the language of his ancestors, the persona is unable to share in those experiences which give families their cohesion, and thereby signal his right to participate as a full-fledged member. Hence, he can only refer now to *lejanos primos* (distant cousins) (I: 398).

Despite their remoteness, he still admits to a relationship with them. However, the years of separation have resulted in an alteration of both modes of perception. Consequently, acts which are performed in the new environment in keeping with what is assumed to be the spirit of the old, often take on a new significance, or undergo a shift in focus. This is noticeable in the sphere of the dance. The rumba, for example, was originally a neo-African secular festival dance which had several movements, and, as with dance forms in Africa, was dramatic in orientation.[20] However, by the time Guillén came to write his poem, *Rumba*, the dramatic focus of the dance was still retained, but the emphasis was now solely on the erotic element, to the exclusion of other sequences such as the *yambú*, which mimed old age:

> Pimienta de la cadera,
> grupa flexible y dorado:
> rumbera buena,
> rumbera mala.

> [Pepper of the hip,
> flexible and golden rump
> good (female) rumba dancer,
> bad (female) rumba dancer.]

(I: 123)

The above comments by the narrator are African in flavor, in that they reveal that the audience is not simply a passive spectator of the performance by the dancing couple. Nevertheless, a new mode of consciousness has intervened, which results in the simplification of the rhythm of the music; as well as the reduction of the various movements of the dance to the single movement of the *guagancó*, an attraction/repulsion dance of courtship.

A similar transformation can be observed in *Ebano real* (*Royal Ebony*), which Olabiyi Yai has aptly defined as a praise peom.[21] Indeed, the poem is structured on the principle of parallelism and repetition, which Ruth Finnegan has observed to be marked features of praise poetry.[22] As is customary in poems of this genre, the first stanza extols the virtues of the tree:

> Te vi al pasar, una tarde,
> ébano, y te saludé:
> duro entre todos los troncos,
> duro entre todos los troncos,
> tu corazón recordé.
>
> Arará, cuévano,
arará sabulú.

> [On passing by one afternoon, I saw you,
> ebony, and I greeted you:
> hard among all trunks,
> hard among all trunks,
> I remembered your heart.
>
> Arará, cuévano,
arará sabulú.]

(I:229)

But in the rest of the poem, a disproportionate number of stanzas are devoted to the pursuit of a reward by the panegyrist:

—Ebano real, yo quiero un barco,
ébano real, de tu negra madera . . .
Ahora no puede ser,
espérate, amigo, espérate,
espérate a que me muera.

[—Royal ebony, I want a boat,
royal ebony, from your black wood . . .
It can't be now,
wait, my friend, wait,
wait until I am dying.]

(I:229)

While there are instances in African literature when the panegyric will include the direct request for a reward from the patron, particularly in the more democratic societies, where the poet has to survive by his own initiative and enterprise rather than through royal patronage,[23] nevertheless, the emphasis there is still on validating and affirming the status of the patron, and not, as in Guillén's poem, on boldly highlighting the profit motive.

In emphasizing the profit motive, perhaps Guillén wishes to convey an idea of the exploitative nature of relationships in the Caribbean. Needless to say, the Americas are not the only area where exploitation occurs, since Africa too has proven vulnerable in that regard. Not only were parts of the continent ravaged in the past to supply workers for the mines and plantations of the New World, but even in the twentieth century, Europe has continued to impose its imperial will on the African continent.

That this is invariably a violent situation is clearly seen from the title of Guillén's poem, *Soldados en Abisinia* (*Soldiers in Abyssinia*). In Mussolini's case, the desire to restore the empire of the Caesars leads to the incorporation of Ethiopia into the Italian sphere of influence. But in Guillén's opinion, this gesture will ultimately be unsuccessful because it is founded upon an abstraction:

El dedo, hijo de César,
penetra el continente:
no hablan las aguas de papel,
ni los desiertos de papel,
ni las ciudades de papel.
El mapa, frío, de papel,

y el dedo, hijo de César,
con la uña sangrienta, ya clavada
sobre una Abisinia de papel.

[His finger, child of Caesar,
pierces the continent:
the paper waters do not speak,
nor do the paper deserts,
nor do the paper cities.
The cold paper map,
and his finger, child of Caesar,
with its bloody nail, already stuck
on a paper Abyssinia.]

(I:185)

In his drive for self-aggrandizement, Mussolini evidently does not take into consideration the possibility of local resistance to this threat to Ethiopian national sovereignty. There is therefore a contrast between the passivity of the "paper Abyssinia" envisaged by Mussolini and the dynamism displayed by a country determined to resist colonial penetration:

Abisinia se encrespa,
se enarca,
grita,
rabia,
protesta.

[Abyssinia gets angry,
becomes confused,
shouts,
rages,
protests.]

(I:186)

By attributing the actions to the country as a whole rather than to individuals, Guillén implies that this is a mass movement for liberation.

Nevertheless, the defensive actions taken by the Ethiopians are clearly ineffectual, even if energetic. But instead of underscoring the Ethiopian defeat, Guillén emphasizes the high cost of victory to Italy in human lives:

Entonces, los soldados
(que no hicieron su viaje sobre un mapa)
los soldados,

lejos de Mussolini,
solos;
los soldados
se abrasarán en el desierto,
y mucho más pequeños, desde luego,
los soldados
irán secándose después lentamente al sol,
los soldados
devueltos
en el excremento de los buitres.

[Then, the soldiers
(who did not travel on a map)
the soldiers,
far from Mussolini,
alone;
the soldiers
will be burnt up in the desert,
and much smaller, of course,
the soldiers
afterwards will go on withering slowly in the sun,
the soldiers
returned
in the excrement of the vultures.]
                    (I:187)

Moreover, for Guillén the Italian-Ethiopian War is not simply a confrontation between colonizer and colonized. It also represents a class conflict within the ranks of the colonizers:

Mussolini, bañado,
fresco,
limpio,
vertiginoso.
Mussolini, contento.
Y serio.

¡Ah, pero los soldados
irán cayendo y tropezando!
Los soldados
no harán su viaje sobre un mapa,
sino sobre el suelo de África,

bajo el sol de África.
Alla no encontrarán ciudades de papel;
las ciudades serán algo más que puntos que hablen
con verdes vocecitas topográficas:
hormigueros de balas,
toses de ametralladoras,
cañaverales de lanzas.

[Mussolini, bathed,
fresh,
clean,
dizzy.
Mussolini, happy.
And serious.

Ah, but the soldiers
will go on falling and stumbling!
The soldiers
will not travel on a map,
but on the soil of Africa,
under the sun of Africa.
There they will not find paper cities;
the cities will be something more than dots that speak
with little green topographical voices:
swarms of bullets,
coughs of machine-guns,
canefields of lances.]

(I:186-87)

By contrasting the cool calculations of Mussolini, who is isolated from the main theater of events, with the harsh realities encountered by his soldiers, Guillén suggests that the Italian soldiers who go to their deaths in Ethiopia are the unwitting executors of a policy which is contrary to their own interests. The implication is that like the Ethiopians, these soldiers are equally victims of a misguided imperialist decision.

If *Soldados en Abisinia* hints at the similarity of conditions among the ranks of the oppressed, and therefore offers the prospect of their potential solidarity, irrespective of race, culture or national origin, *Mau-Mau* is exclusively concerned with advocating self-determination for the African victims of colonial oppression. Guillén reveals the Mau Mau to be engaged in an unequal combat against the British settlers, who, supported by their govern-

ment, use their military and technological superiority, as well as their control
of the print media, to overwhelm the Kikuyu fighters physically and psy-
chologically. Dual interpretations of the same event reflect the existence of
a compartmentalized colonial world, "inhabited by two different species,"
already described by Fanon:[24]

Envenenada tinta
habla de los mau-maus;
negros de diente y uña,
de antropofagia y totem.
Gruñe la tinta, cuenta,
dice que los mau-maus
mataron a un inglés . . .
(Aquí en secreto: era
el mismo inglés de kepis
profanador, de rifle
civilizado y remington,
que en el pulmón de África
con golpe seco y firme
clavó su daga-imperio,
de hierro abecedario,
de sífilis, de pólvora,
de money, business, yes.)

[Poisoned ink
speaks of the Mau Mau
blacks of tooth and nail,
of anthropophagy and totem.
The ink grunts, relates,
says that the Mau Mau
killed an Englishman . . .
(Confidentially speaking: it was
the same Englishman with the violating
shako, with civilized
rifle and Remington,
who in the lung of Africa
with a dry, firm stroke
stuck his dagger-empire,
of alphabet iron,
of syphilis gunpowder,
of money, business, yes.)]

(II:32)

The fundamental conflict of interests lends to seemingly absurd gestures on the part of the Mau Mau:

> Tinta de largas letras
> cuenta que los mau-maus
> arrasan como un río
> salvaje las cosechas,
> envenenan las aguas,
> queman las tierras próvidas,
> matan toros y ciervos.
> (Aquí en secreto: eran
> dueños de diez mil chozas,
> del árbol, de la lluvia,
> del sol, de la montaña,
> dueños de la semilla,
> del surco, de la nube,
> del viento, de la paz . . .)
>
> Algo sencillo y simple
> ¡oh inglés de duro kepis!
> simple y sencillo: dueños.
>
> [Long-typed ink
> tells that the Mau Mau
> wreck the harvests
> like a savage river,
> poison the waters,
> burn the productive lands,
> kill bulls and deer.
> (Confidentially speaking: they were
> owners of ten thousand huts,
> of the tree, of the rain,
> of the sun, of the mountain,
> owners of the seed,
> of the furrow, of the cloud,
> of the wind, of peace . . .
>
> Something plain and simple
> Oh Englishman with the hard shako!
> simple and plain: owners.]

                    (II:33-34)

But the apparently illogical "strategy of immediacy"[25] that they adopt is in fact a dramatization of their need for a more just sociopolitical order.

Through their disruption of the agricultural economy, they are manifesting their refusal to participate in a system that ascribes to them a permanently inferior status. In attempting to negate the conditions of existence defined for them by the British other, the Mau Mau have taken the first step in what René Depestre would define as a process of "dezombification,"[26] as they strive to recover the land and liberty alienated from them by the British.

It is significant that Guillén refers to the group by the name, "Mau Mau," which, according to Kenneth Grundy, was never used by its members to designate themselves, but rather was a term "more generally employed by Europeans, their governments, and their press."[27] By a technique of ironic reversal, already studied by Antonio Ollíz Boyd in another context, [28] Guillén gives this originally derogatory term a more positive valorization by revealing the British to be capable of far greater savagery than the Kikuyu whom they denounce:

> Letras de larga tinta
> cuentan que los mau-maus
> casas de sueño y trópico
> británicas tomaron
> y a fuego, sangre, muerte,
> bajo el asalto bárbaro
> cien ingleses cayeron . . . .
> (Aquí en secreto: eran
> los mismos cien ingleses
> a quienes Londres dijo:
> —Matad, comed mau-maus;
> barred, incendiad Kenya;
> que ni un solo kikuyus
> viva, y que sus mujeres
> por siempre de ceniza
> servida vean su mesa
> y seco vean su vientre.)

> [Abundant-inked type
> relate that the Mau Mau
> took British tropical
> dream houses
> and by fire, blood, death,
> under the barbarous assault
> one hundred Englishmen fell . . .
> (Confidentially speaking: they were

the same one hundred Englishmen
to whom London said:
—Kill, eat Mau Mau;
sweep away, burn Kenya;
let not a single Kikuyu
live, and let their women
see their tables
forever served with ashes
and their wombs barren.)]

                                                    (II:32-33)

What the British perceive as a "constitutional depravity"[29] in the nature of the Mau Mau is thereby revealed to be a political response to a situation which denies the Kikuyu the right to be.

If Guillén's ethnic background, as well as the sociocultural composition of contemporary Cuba, serve to maintain his interest in the problems of twentieth-century Africa, there is no doubt that for him, the historical process is irreversible. While he acknowledges the continuity of the past in the present, he projects a vision of Africa that is not entirely situated in the mythical dimension but is also subject to the forces of contingency. Hence the multiplicity of African images evident in his work. The manifestation of the African presence displayed by the *Balada del güije* (*Ballad of the River-Spirit*) coexists with a lament for its absence in *El apellido* (*The Family Name*), while the stereotypical portrait of the primitive African appears side by side with its polar opposite in *Mau-Maus*, and the timeless, landless perception of the *Balada de los dos abuelos* (*Ballad of the Two Grandfathers*) exists alongside of the particularistic, historical version of *Soldados en Abisinia (Soldiers in Abyssinia)*. Racial heritage, as well as common human experiences and ideals, make it possible for the poet to capture the African continent in a variety of attitudes. But cognizant of the effects of time and history, Guillén's interpretation is grounded in a recognition of his own difference. Hence there is no attempt at a facile identification. The essential perspective on Africa remains that of "a Yoruba from Cuba."

NOTES

1. M. G. Smith, "The African Heritage in the Caribbean," in *Caribbean Studies: A Symposium*, ed. Vera Rubin (Seattle, 1960), p. 40.

2. Citations are from Nicolás Guillén, *Obra poética, 1920-1972*, 2 vols. (Havana, 1974), and are given in the text parenthetically. All translations are by the author.

3. Regarding Yoruba supremacy in Cuba, see Salvador Bueno, "'La canción del bongo': Sobre la cultura mulata de Cuba," *Cuadernos Americanos* 206 (May-June 1976): 97.

4. For Shango's attributes see William Bascom, *Shango in the New World* (Austin, Texas, 1972), pp. 14-15.

5. On the necessity of feeding the god, so as to transmit his protective power to the worshiper, see William R. Bascom, "The Focus of Cuban Santería," in *Peoples and Cultures of the Caribbean*, ed. Michael M. Horowitz (Garden City, N.Y., 1971), pp. 523-25. Regarding the need for protective charms to be recharged periodically see John S. Mbiti, *African Religions and Philosophy* (New York, 1969), p. 199.

6. Mbiti, *African Religions*, p. 77.

7. On the mystical power of the word, see Mbiti, *African Religions*, p. 197.

8. For the idea that African music is conceived vocally, see John Storm Roberts, *Black Music of Two Worlds* (New York, 1974), p. 6. For the stylistic features of African music, see Richard Alan Waterman, "African Influence on the Music of the Americas," in *Acculturation in the Americas*, ed. Sol Tax (New York, 1967), pp. 207-18.

9. Ruth Finnegan, *Oral Literature in Africa* (London, 1970), p. 265.

10. G. R. Coulthard, *Race and Colour in Caribbean Literature* (London, 1962), pp. 27-29.

11. O. R. Dathorne, *The Black Mind: A History of African Literature* (Minneapolis, 1974), pp. 437-40.

12. Cf. Christopher Fyfe, "The Dynamics of African Dispersal: The Transatlantic Slave Trade," in *The African Diaspora*, ed. Martin L. Kilson and Robert Rotberg (Cambridge, 1976), pp. 57-74; Joseph C. Miller, "The Slave Trade in Congo and Angola," in Kilson and Rotberg, *The African Diaspora*, pp. 75-113; G. J. Afolabi Ojo, *Yoruba Culture: A Geographical Analysis* (London, 1966), pp. 108-22; Walter Rodney, "African Slavery and Other Forms of Social Oppression on the Upper Guinea Coast in the Context of the Atlantic Slave Trade," *The Journal of African History* 7 (1966): 431-43; idem, *West Africa and the Atlantic Slave-Trade* (Nairobi, 1969).

13. Lloyd King, "Mr. Black in Cuba," *African Studies Association of the West Indies Bulletin*, 5 (1972): 25-26.

14. Edward Kamau Brathwaite, "The African Presence in Caribbean Literature," in *Slavery, Colonialism, and Racism*, ed. S. W. Mintz (New York, 1974), pp. 80-82.

15. Fernando Ortiz, *Hampa afro-cubana: Los negros brujos (apuntes para un estudio de etnología criminal)* (Madrid, 1917), p. 353. For an analysis of Cuba's late development as a plantation society, which would explain the presence of native Africans there in the twentieth century, see Franklin W. Knight, *Slave Society in Cuba in the Nineteenth Century* (Madison, Wis., 1970).

16. George Lamming, "Actitudes de la literatura antillana con respecto á Africa," *Casa de las Americas* 56 (September-October 1969): 120-25.

17. George Lamming, *The Pleasures of Exile* (London, 1960), p. 160 (hereafter cited as *Exile*).

18. My italics.

19. Lamming, *Exile*, p. 160.

20. Roberts, *Black Music*, pp. 95-96.

21. Olabiyi Yai, "Influence Yoruba dans la poésie Cubaine: Nicolás Guillén et la tradition poétique Yoruba" (Seminar Paper, Department of Modern European Languages, University of Ife, Nigeria, 1975, pp. 14-15. I am indebted to Maureen Warner Lewis for providing me with a copy of this paper.

22. Finnegan, *Oral Literature*, p. 131.

23. Ibid., pp. 92-96.

24. Frantz Fanon, *The Wretched of the Earth*, trans. Constance Farrington (New York, 1963), pp. 38-40.

25. Ibid., p. 132.

26. René Depestre, "Los fundamentos socioculturales de nuestra identidad," *Casa de las Américas* 58 (January-February 1970): 27.

27. Kenneth W. Grundy, *Guerrilla Struggle in Africa: An Analysis and Preview* (New York, 1971), pp. 78-79.

28. Antonio Olliz Boyd, "The Concept of Black Awareness as a Thematic Approach in Latin American Literature," in *Blacks in Hispanic Literature: Critical Essays*, ed. Miriam Decosta (Port Washington, N. Y., 1977), p. 66.

29. Fanon, *Wretched of the Earth*, p. 42.

SELECTED BIBLIOGRAPHY

Abrahams, Roger. "Pull Out Your Purse and Pay." *Folklore* 79 (1968): 176-201.

Achebe, Chinua. *Arrow of God*. London, 1964.

Adamson, Alan H. "The Reconstruction of Plantation Labor after Emancipation: The Case of British Guiana." In *Race and Slavery in the Western Hemisphere: Quantitative Studies*, edited by Stanley L. Engerman and Eugene D. Genovese. Princeton, N.J., 1975.

Afolabi Ojo, G. J. *Yoruba Culture: A Geographical Analysis*. London, 1966.

Alleyne, Mervyn. "The Linguistic Continuity of Africa in the Caribbean." *Black Academy Review* 1 (Winter 1970): 3-16.

Allsopp, Richard. *Dictionary of Jamaican English*. San Juan, Puerto Rico, 1970.

Alvárez Nazario, Manuel. *El elemento afro-negroide en el español de Puerto Rico: Contribución al estudio del negro en América*. San Juan, Puerto Rico, 1967.

_____. *El influjo indígena en el español de Puerto Rico*. San Juan, Puerto Rico, 1977.

Anstey, Roger. *The Atlantic Slave Trade and the British Abolition, 1760-1810*. Atlantic Highlands, N.J., 1975.

_____. "The Volume and Profitability of the British Slave Trade, 1761-1807." In *Race and Slavery in the Western Hemisphere,* edited by Stanley L. Engerman and Eugene D. Genovese. Princeton, N.J., 1975.

Ardener, Edwin. "Lineage and Locality among the Mba-Ise-Ibo." *Africa* 29 (1959): 113-33.

Asein, Samuel. "The Concept of Form: A Study of Some Ancestral Elements in Brathwaite's Trilogy." *African Studies Association of the West Indies Bulletin* 4 (1971): 9-38.

Asiegbu, J. *Slavery and the Politics of Liberation, 1787-1861: A Study of Liberated African Emigration and British Anti-Slavery Policy.* London, 1970.

Ata Aidoo, Ana. "Akan and English." *West Africa* (21 September 1968), p. 1099.

Balandier, Georges. *La vie quotidienne au royaume de Kongo du XVIe au XVIIIe siècles.* Paris, 1965.

Barclay, Alexander. *A Practical View of the Present State of Slavery.* London, 1823.

Barnet, Miguel. *The Autobiography of a Runaway Slave: Esteban Montejo.* New York, 1968.

Barrett, Leonard E. *The Rastafarians: A Study in Messianic Cultism in Jamaica.* Caribbean Monograph Series 6. Rio Piedras, Puerto Rico, 1968.

Bascom, William R. "The Focus of Cuban Santería." In *Peoples and Cultures of the Caribbean*, edited by Michael M. Horowitz. Garden City, N.Y., 1971.

_____. *Shango in the New World.* Austin, Texas, 1972.

_____. *The Yoruba of Southwestern Nigeria.* New York, 1969.

Beckwith, Martha W. *Black Roadways: A Study of Jamaican Folk Life.* Chapel Hill, N.C., 1929.

_____. *Christmas Mummings in Jamaica.* New York, 1923.

_____. *Jamaica Folklore.* New York, 1928.

Bettelheim, Judith. "The Jonkonnu Festival." *Jamaica Journal* 10 (1976): 20-27.

Blainey, Geoffrey. *The Tyranny of Distance: How Distance Shaped Australia's History.* London, 1975.

Bolton, H. Carrington. "Gombay: A Festival Rite of Bermudian Negroes." *Journal of American Folklore* 3 (1890): 2.

Brathwaite, Edward Kamau. "The African Presence in Caribbean Literature." *Daedalus.* 103 (Spring 1974): 73-109.

_____. "Caliban, Ariel, and Unprospero in the Conflict of Creolization: A Study of the Slave Revolt in Jamaica in 1831-32." In *Comparative Perspectives on Slavery in New World Plantation Societies*, edited by Vera Rubin and Arthur Tuden. New York, 1977.

_____. *Contradictory Omens, Cultural Diversity and Integration in the Caribbean.* Kingston, Jamaica, 1974.

————. *The Development of Creole Society in Jamaica, 1770-1820*. Oxford, 1971.

————. *Islands*. New York, 1969.

————. *Rites of Passage*. New York, 1967.

Brown, Beverly. "George Liele: Black Baptist and Pan Africanist, 1750-1826." *Savacou* 11/12 (September 1975): 58-67.

Buchner, J. H. *The Moravians in Jamaica, History of the Mission of the United Brethrens' Church to the Negroes in the Island of Jamaica, from the Year 1754 to 1854*. London, 1854.

Bueno, Salvador. " 'La canción del bongo': Sobre la cultura mulata de Cuba." *Cuadernos Americanos* 206 (May-June 1976): 96-101.

Cabrera, Lydia. *Anagó, Vocabulario Lucumí*. Havana, 1957.

————. *El Monte*. 2d ed. Miami, 1968.

————. *La sociedad secreta Abakuá: narrada por viejos adeptos*. Miami, 1970.

————. *Otán Iyebiyé: las piedras preciosas*. Miami, 1970.

————. *Refranes de negros viejos*. Miami, 1970.

Cassidy, Frank. "Jamaican Creole and Twi: Some Comparisons." Paper presented at the Conference on Creole Languages and Educational Development. Trinidad, 1971.

Cassidy, Frederick G. *Dictionary of Jamaican English*. Cambridge, England, 1970.

Comitas, Lambros, and Lowenthal, David, eds. *Slaves, Free Men, Citizens: West Indian Perspectives*. New York, 1973.

————. *Work and Family Life*. New York, 1973.

Cook, Sherburne F., and Borah, Woodrow. *Essays in Population History: Mexico and the Caribbean*. 2 vols. Berkeley, Cal., 1971-74.

————. *The Population of the Mixteca Alta*. Berkeley, Cal., 1968. Coulthard, G. R. *Race and Colour in Caribbean Literature*. London, 1962.

Craton, Michael M. *Searching for the Invisible Man: Slaves and Plantation Life in Jamaica*. Cambridge, Mass., 1978.

Crowley, Daniel. "The Midnight Robbers." *Caribbean Quarterly* 4 (1956): 263-74.

Cundall, Frank, and Anderson, Izett, eds. *Jamaica Proverbs and Sayings*. 2d ed. London, 1927. Reprinted. Kingston, Jamaica, 1972.

Curry, Robert. *Bahamian Lore*. Paris, 1928.

Curtin, Philip D., ed. *Africa Remembered*. Madison, Wis., 1967.

————. *The Atlantic Slave Trade: A Census*. Madison, Wis., 1969.

————. "Measuring the Atlantic Slave Trade." In *Race and Slavery in the Western Hemisphere: Quantitative Studies*, edited by Stanley L.

Engerman and Eugene D. Genovese. Princeton, N.J., 1975.

————. *Two Jamaicas: The Role of Ideas in a Tropical Colony, 1830-1865*. New York, 1955. Reprint ed. New York, 1970.

Daaku, Kwame Yeba. *Trade and Politics on the Gold Coast, 1600-1720*. Oxford, 1970.

Dalby, David. "Ashanti Survivals in the Language and Traditions of the Windward Maroons of Jamaica." *African Language Studies* 12 (1971): 31-51.

Dathorne, O. R. "Africa in West Indian Literature." *Black Orpheus* 16 (1964): 42-54.

————. *The Black Mind: A History of African Literature*. Minneapolis, Minn., 1974.

Dawes, Neville. *The Last Enchantment*. London, 1960.

D'Costa, Jean, and Berry, Jack. "Some Considerations of Tone in Jamaican Creole." Paper presented to the Conference on Caribbean Linguistics, Jamaica, 1971.

DeCamp, David. "The Development of Pidgin and Creole Studies." In *Symposium on Cultural Identity of French-Speaking in the Americas*, edited by Albert Valdman. Bloomington, Indiana, 1977: 3-20.

De Costa, Miriam, ed. *Blacks in Hispanic Literature: Critical Essays*. Port Washington, N.Y., 1977.

de Craemer, Willy; Vansina, Jan; and Fox, Renée C. "Religious Movements in Central Africa: A Theoretical Study." *Comparative Studies in Society and History* 18 (October 1976): 458-75.

Defries, Amelia. *The Fortunate Islands*. London, 1929.

del Monte y Tejada, Antonio. *Historia de Santo Domingo*. 4 vols. Santo Domingo, 1890.

Denevan, William M. *The Native Population of the Americas in 1492*. Madison, Wis., 1976.

Depestre, René. "Los fundamentos socioculturales de nuestra identidad." *Casa de las Américas* 58 (January/February 1970).

Deschamps Chapeaux, Pedro. "El lenguaje Abakuá." *Etnología y Folklore* 4 (1967): 39-48.

Dirks, Robert, and Kearns, Virginia. *National Studies* 3 (1975).

Dookhan, Isaac. "A History of the British Virgin Islands." Ph.D. dissertation, University of the West Indies, Jamaica, 1968.

Douglas, Mary. *Purity and Danger*. New York, 1966.

Drayton, Arthur. "West Indian Consciousness in West Indian Verse: A Historical Perspective." *Journal of Commonwealth Literature* 9 (July 1970): 66-88.

Eltis, David. "The Traffic in Slaves between the British West Indies Colonies,

1807-1833." *Economic History Review* 25 (February 1972): 55-64.

Engerman, Stanley L., and Genovese, Eugene D., eds. *Race and Slavery in the Western Hemisphere: Quantitative Studies.* Princeton, N.J., 1975.

Equiano, Olaudah. *Equiano's Travels: The Interesting Life of Olaudah Equiano, or Gustavus Vassa, the African.* London, 1789.

Fanon, Frantz. *Black Skin, White Masks.* New York, 1967.

————. *The Wretched of the Earth.* Translated by Constance Farrington. New York, 1963.

Finnegan, Ruth. *Oral Literature in Africa.* London. 1970.

Fyfe, Christopher. "The Dynamics of African Dispersal: The Trans-Atlantic Slave Trade." In *The African Diaspora: Interpretive Essays*, edited by Martin L. Kilson and Robert I. Rotberg. Cambridge, Mass., 1976.

Gardner, W. J. *A History of Jamaica.* London, 1971.

Godet, Theodore. *Bermuda.* London, 1860.

González-Wippler, Migene. *Santería: African Magic in Latin America.* New York, 1975.

Green, William A. *British Slave Emancipation: The Sugar Colonies and the Great Experiment, 1830-1865.* Oxford, 1976.

Grundy, Kenneth W. *Guerrilla Struggle in Africa: An Analysis and Preview.* New York, 1971.

Guillén, Nicolás. *Obra poética, 1920-1972.* 2 vols. Havana, 1974.

Gutman, Herbert. *The Black Family in Slavery and Freedom, 1750-1925.* New York, 1976.

Hall, Douglas. *Free Jamaica, 1838-1865: An Economic History.* 2d. ed. London. 1969.

Hall, Robert. "Creolized Languages and 'Genetic Relationships.' " *Word* 14 (1958): 367-73.

Hancock, Ian. "A Provisional Comparison of the English-Based Atlantic Creoles." In *Pidginization and Creolization of Languages*, edited by Dell Hymes. New York, 1971.

Handler, Jerome S. "The Amerindian Slave Population of Barbados in the Seventeenth and Early Eighteenth Centuries." *Caribbean Studies* 8 (1969): 38-64.

Handler, Jerome S., and Lange, Frederick W. *Plantation Slavery in Barbados.* Cambridge, Mass., 1978.

Harris, Wilson. *Tradition, the Writer and Society.* London, 1967.

Henriques, Fernando. *Family and Colour in Jamaica.* London, 1953.

Herskovits, Melville J. *The Myth of the Negro Past.* Boston, Mass., 1941.

Herskovits, Melville J., and Herskovits, Frances S. *Trinidad Village.* New York, 1964.

Higman, Barry W. "Household Structure and Fertility on Jamaican Slave Plantations: A Nineteenth Century Example." *Population Studies* 27 (1973): 527-50.

_____. *Slave Population and Economy in Jamaica, 1807-1833*. Cambridge, England, 1976.

Hill, Errol. *The Trinidad Carnival: Mandate for a National Theatre*. Austin, Texas, 1972.

Hoetink, Harry. "Formas de organización familiar en el Caribe" *Sonderhefte, Colegium Humboldtianum*. Bielefeld, West Germany, 1971.

_____. *Het patroon van de oude Curaçaose samenliving*. Assen, Netherlands, 1958.

_____. "Resource Competition, Monopoly, and Socioracial Diversity." In *Ethnicity and Resource Competition in Plural Societies*, edited by Leo A. Despres. The Hague, 1975.

_____. *Slavery and Race Relations in the Americas: An Inquiry into Their Nature and Nexus*. New York, 1973.

Horowitz, Michael M., ed. *Peoples and Cultures of the Caribbean*. Garden City, N.Y., 1971.

Hurault, Jean. *Africains de Guyane: La vie matérielle et l'art des Noirs refugies de Guyane*. The Hague, 1970.

Huttar, George. "Some Kwa-Like Features of Djuka Syntax." Paper presented at the Summer Institute of Linguistics, Australia, 1974.

Hymes, Dell, ed. *Pidginization and Creolization of Languages*. New York, 1971.

Isichei, Elizabeth. *A History of the Ibo People*. New York, 1976.

Jones, Rhett S., and Dzidzienyo, Anani. "Social Structure and Racial Ideologies in New York." Paper presented at the Conference on the African Mind in New York. Rutgers University, N.J. 1976.

Kerr, Madeline. *Personality and Conflict in Jamaica*. Liverpool, 1963.

Kilson, Martin L., and Rotberg, Robert I., eds. *The African Diaspora: Interpretive Essays*. Cambridge, Mass., 1976.

King, Lloyd. "Mr. Black in Cuba." *African Studies Association of the West Indies Bulletin* 5 (1972): 25-26.

Klein, Herbert S., and Engerman, Stanley L. "Fertility Differentials between Slaves in the United States and the British West Indies: A Note on Lactation Practices and their Possible Implications." *William and Mary Quarterly*. Third Series, 35 (April, 1978): 357-74.

Knight, Franklin W. *The African Dimension in Latin American Societies*. New York, 1974.

————. *The Caribbean: The Genesis of a Fragmented Nationalism.* New York, 1978.

————. "Patterns of Colonial Society and Culture: Latin America and the Caribbean, 1492-1804." In *South Atlantic Studies,* edited by Jack R. Censer, N. Steven Steinert, and Amy M. McCandles. vol. 2, Charleston, S.C., 1978.

————. *Slave Society in Cuba in the Nineteenth Century.* Madison, Wis., 1970.

Laman, Kar. *The Kongo.* 3 vols. Lund, 1962.

Lamming, George. "Actitudes de la literatura antillana con respecto a Africa." *Casa de las Américas* 56 (September/October 1969): 120-25.

————. "Caribbean Literature: The Black Rock of Africa." *African Forum* 1 (Spring 1966): 32-52.

————. *The Pleasures of Exile.* London, 1960.

————. *Season of Adventure.* London, 1960.

Laroche, Maximilien. "The Myth of the Zombi." In *Exile and Tradition: Studies in African and Caribbean Literature,* edited by Roland Smith, pp. 41-61. Halifax, Nova Scotia, 1976.

Larrazabal Blanco, Carlos. *Los negros y la esclavitud en Santo Domingo,* 1967.

Lawton, David. "Tone and Jamaican Creole." Paper presented to the Conference on Caribbean Linguistics, Jamaica, 1971.

Leith-Ross, Sylvia. *African Women: A Study of the Ibo of Nigeria.* London, 1939.

Lewis, M. G. (Monk). *Journal of a West Indian Proprietor.* London, 1834.

Lloyd, P. C., ed. "Osifekunde of Ijebu." In *Africa Remembered,* edited by Philip D. Curtin. Madison, Wis., 1967.

Lloyd, Susette H. *Sketches of Bermuda.* London, 1835.

Long, Edward. *The History of Jamaica.* 3 vols. London, 1970.

Lowenthal, David, and Comitas, Lambros, eds. *The Aftermath of Sovereignty: West Indian Perspectives.* New York, 1973.

————. *Consequences of Class and Color: West Indian Perspectives.* New York, 1975.

MacDonald, John S., and MacDonald, Leatrice D. "Transformation of African and Indian Family Traditions in the South Caribbean." *Comparative Studies in Society and History* 15 (1973): 171-98.

March, Bertha. *Bermuda Days.* London, 1929.

Martin, Dolores M. "Close Encounters of the Third World." *The Washington Post Book World.* 22 January 1978, p. 1.

Martinez-Alier, Verena. *Marriage, Class and Colour in Nineteenth-Century*

Cuba: A Study of Racial and Sexual Values in a Slave Society. Cambridge, England, 1974.

Mason, Philip. *Prospero's Magic: Some Thoughts on Class and Race.* London, 1962.

Mbiti, John S. *African Religions and Philosophy.* New York, 1970.

McCallan, E. A. *Life in Old St. Davids.* Bermuda, 1948.

McKay, Claude. *Banana Bottom.* New York, 1933.

McLaughlin, E. C. "Gombeys and Casave Pie." *The Bermudian* (December 1932): 1.

Mellafe, Rolando. *La introducción de la esclavitud negra en Chile: Tráfico y rutas.* Santiago, Chile, 1959.

Metraux, Alfred. *Voodoo in Haiti.* New York, 1972.

Miers, Suzanne, and Kopytoff, Igor. *Slavery in Africa: Historical and Anthropological Perspectives.* Madison, Wis., 1977.

Miller, Joseph C. "The Slave Trade in Congo and Angola." In *The African Diaspora: Interpretive Essays*, edited by Martin L. Kilson and Robert I. Rotberg. Cambridge, Mass., 1976.

Millette, James. *The Genesis of Crown Colony Government: Trinidad 1783-1810.* Curepe, Trinidad, 1970.

Mintz, Sidney W. "Caribbean Nationhood in Anthropological Perspective." In *Caribbean Integration: Papers on Social and Political and Economic Integration*, edited by Sybil Lewis and Thomas G. Mathews. Rio Piedras, Puerto Rico, 1967.

————. *Caribbean Transformations.* Chicago, 1974.

————. "Labor and Sugar in Puerto Rico and Jamaica: 1800-1850." *Comparative Studies in Society and History* 2 (1959): 273-83.

————. *Slavery, Colonialism, and Racism.* New York, 1974.

Mintz, Sidney W., and Price, Richard. *An Anthropological Approach to the Afro-American Past: A Caribbean Perspective.* Philadelphia, 1976.

Monod, Jacques. *Chance and Necessity: An Essay on the Natural Philosophy of Modern Biology.* New York, 1971.

Moore, Joseph G. "Religion of Jamaica Negroes: A Study of Afro-Jamaican Acculturation." Ph.D. dissertation, Northwestern University, 1953.

Moreno Fraginals, Manuel, ed. *Africa en América Latina.* Mexico City, 1977.

————. "Africa in Cuba: A Quantitative Analysis of the African Population in the Island of Cuba." In *Comparative Perspectives on Slavery in New World Plantation Societies*, edited by Vera Rubin and Arthur Tuden. New York, 1977.

————. *The Sugarmill: The Socioeconomic Complex of Sugar in Cuba.* New York, 1976.

Moya Pons, Frank. *La Española en el siglo XVI*. Santiago de los Caballeros, Dominican Republic, 1971.

Murdock, George P. *Africa: Its Peoples and Their Cultural History*. New York, 1959.

Murray, D.R. "Statistics of the Slave Trade to Cuba, 1790-1867." *Journal of Latin American Studies* 3 (1971): 131-49.

Nettleford, Rex. *Mirror, Mirror*. Kingston, 1970.

Nsugbe, Philip O. *Ohaffia: A Matrilineal Ibo People*. Oxford, 1974.

Ola Oke, David. "On the Genesis of New World Black English." *Caribbean Quarterly* 23 (March 1977): 61-79.

Oliver, Lord. *Jamaica: The Blessed Isle*. London, 1936.

Olliz Boyd, Antonio. "The Concept of Black Awareness as a Thematic Approach in Latin American Literature." In *Blacks in Hispanic Literature: Critical Essays*, edited by Miriam De Costa. Port Washington, N.Y., 1977.

Olmstead, David. "Comparative Notes on Yoruba and Lucumí." *Language* 29 (1953): 157-64.

Ortiz, Fernando. *Hampa afro-cubana: Los negros brujos (apuntes para un estudio de etnología criminal)*. Madrid, 1971.

Palmer, Colin A. *Slaves of the White God: Blacks in Mexico, 1570-1650*. Cambridge, Mass., 1976.

Parrinder, Geoffrey. *West African Religion: A Study of Beliefs and Practices of the Akan, Ewe, Yoruba, Ibo and Kindred Peoples*. London, 1961.

Parsons, Alan. *A Winter in Paradise*. London, 1926.

Patterson, Orlando. "From Endo-deme to Matri-deme: An Interpretation of the Development of Kinship and Social Organization Among the Slaves of Jamaica, 1655-1830." In *Eighteenth Century Florida and the Caribbean*, edited by Samuel Procter. Gainesville, Fla., 1976.

————. *The Sociology of Slavery: An Analysis of the Origins, Development and Structure of Negro Slave Society in Jamaica*. London, 1967.

Pérez de la Riva, Juan. *Para la historia de la gente sin historia*. Barcelona, 1976.

Phillippo, James M. *Jamaica, Its Past and Present State*. London, 1843.

Phillips, Arthur, ed. *Survey of African Marriage and Family Life*. London, 1953.

Price, Richard. "Caribbean Fishing and Fisherman: A Historical Sketch." *American Anthropologist* 68 (1966): 1363-84.

————. "Kikoongo and Saramaccan: A Reappraisal." *Journal of African Languages* 12 (1973).

————, ed. *Maroon Societies: Rebel Slave Communities in the Americas*. Garden City, N.Y., 1973.

Price, Richard, and Price, Sally. "Saramaka Onomastics: An Afro-American Naming System." *Ethnology* 11 (1972): 341-67.

Rawick, George P., ed. *God Struck Me Dead*. Vol. 19 of *The American Slave: A Composite Autobiography*. 19 vols. Westport, Conn., 1972.

Reckord, Mary. "The Slave Rebellion of 1831." *Jamaica Journal* 3 (June 1959): 25-31.

Roberts, John Storm. *Black Music of Two Worlds*. New York, 1974.

Rodman, Hyman. *Lower Class Families: The Culture of Poverty in Negro Trinidad*. London, 1971.

Rodney, Walter. "African Slavery and Other Froms of Social Oppression on the Upper Guinea Coast in the Context of the Atlantic Slave Trade." *The Journal of African History* 7 (1966): 431-43.

————. *West Africa and the Atlantic Slave Trade*. Nairobi, 1969.

Rosenblat, Angel. *La población de América en 1492: Viejos y nuevos cálculos*. Mexico City, 1967.

————. "The Population of Hispaniola at the Time of Columbus." In *The Native Population of the Americas in 1492*, edited by William M. Denevan. Madison, Wis., 1976.

Rubin, Vera, and Tuden, Arthur, eds. *Comparative Perspectives on Slavery in New World Plantation Societies*. New York, 1977.

Rubenstein, Hymie. "Diachronic Inference and the Pattern of Lower Class Afro-Caribbean Marriage." *Social and Economic Studies* 26 (1977): 202-16.

Saco, José Antonio. *Historia de las esclavitud de la raza africana en el mundo nuevo y en especial en los paises américo-hispanos*. Havana, 1938.

Salkey, Andrew. *Anancy's Score*. London, 1973.

Sauer, Carl. *The Early Spanish Main*. Berkeley, Cal., 1966.

Schuler, Monica. "Akan Slave Rebellions in the British Caribbean." *Savacou* 1 (1970): 8-31.

————. "Ethnic Slave Rebellions in the Caribbean and the Guianas." *Journal of Social History* 3 (1970): 474-85.

————. " 'Yerri, Yerri, Koongo': A Social History of Liberated African Immigration into Jamaica, 1841-1867." Ph.D. dissertation, University of Wisconsin, 1977.

Scott, Michael. *Tom Cringle's Log*. London, 1833.

Seaga, Edward. "Parent-Teacher Relationships in a Jamaican Village." In *Consequences of Class and Color: West Indian Perspectives*, edited by David Lowenthal and Lambros Comitas. New York, 1975.

Sibley, Inez Knibb. *The Baptists of Jamaica, 1793-1965*. Kingston, Jamaica, 1965.

Simpson, George Eaton. "Religions of the Caribbean." In *The African Diaspora: Interpretive Essays*, edited by Martin L. Kilson and Robert I. Rotberg. Cambridge, Mass., 1976.

————. "The Shango Cult in Nigeria and Trinidad." *American Anthropologist* 64 (December 1962): 1204-19.

Smith, M. G. "The African Heritage in the Caribbean." In *Caribbean Studies: A Symposium*, edited by Vera Rubin. Seattle, Washington, 1960.

————. *Kinship and Community in Carriacou*. New Haven, Conn., 1962.

————. *West Indian Family Structure*. Seattle, Washington, 1962.

Smith, Raymond T. "Religion in the Formation of West Indian Society: Guyana and Jamaica." In *The African Diaspora: Interpretive Essays*, edited by Martin L. Kilson and Robert I. Rotberg. Cambridge, Mass., 1976.

Smith, Roland, ed. *Exile and Tradition: Studies in African and Caribbean Literature*. Halifax, Nova Scotia, 1976.

Steward, Julian. *Handbook of South American Indians*. 7 vols. Washington, D.C. 5 (1949): 655-68.

Taylor, Douglas N. "The Caribs of Dominica." *Smithsonian Institution Bulletin 119: Anthropological Papers*. Washington, D.C. (1938): 103-60.

————. "The Origin of West Indian Creole Languages in Evidence from Grammatical Categories." *American Anthropologist* 65 (1963): 800-814.

Tax, Sol, ed. *Acculturation in the Americas*. New York, 1967.

Thomas, J. J. *Froudacity: West Indian Fables by James Anthony Froude*. London, 1969.

Thomas, M. E. *Jamaica and Voluntary Laborers from Africa, 1840-1865*. Gainesville, Fla., 1974.

Thompson, Robert. "A Note on Some Possible Affinities between the Creole Dialects of the Old World and Those of the New." *Creole Language Studies* 2 (1961): 107-13.

Uchendu, Victor C. *The Igbo of Southeast Nigeria*. New York, 1965.

Verlinden, Charles. "Le 'repartimientó' de Rodrigo de Albuquerque á Espagnola en 1514: Aux origines d'une importante institution économico-sociale de]'empire colonial espagnol." *Mélanges offerts a G. Jacquemyns*. Brussels, 1968. pp. 633-46.

Vila Vilar, Enriqueta. *Hispanoamérica y el comercio de esclavos: Los asientos portugueses*. Seville, 1977.

————. "Los asientos Portugueses y el contrabando de Negros." *Anuario de Estudios Americanos* 30 (1973): 557-609.

Waddell, Hope Masterton. *Twenty-Nine Years in the West Indies and Central Africa*. London, 1863.

Warner Lewis, Maureen. "Odomankoma 'Kyerema Se . . . " *Caribbean Quarterly* 19 (June 1973): 51-99.

Waterman, Richard A. "The African Influence on the Music of the Americas." In *Acculturation in the Americas*, edited by Sol Tax. New York, 1967.

Williams, Cynric R. *A Tour Through the Island of Jamaica*. London, 1827.

Williams, Eric. *Capitalism and Slavery*. Chapel Hill, N.C., 1944.

Wood, Donald. *Trinidad in Transition*. London, 1968.

Wynter, Sylvia. *Hills of Hebron*. New York, 1962.

Yai, Olabiyi. "Influence Yoruba dans la poésie Cubaine: Nicholás Guillén et la tradition poétique Yoruba." Seminar Paper presented to the Department of Modern European Languages, University of Ife, Nigeria, 1975.

Yemitan, Oladipo, ed. *Ijala-Are Ode*. Lagos, Nigeria, 1963.

NOTES ON CONTRIBUTORS

JUDITH BETTELHEIM studied the history of art at Yale University with Robert Farris Thompson. She has taught at the University of California at Berkeley, and is presently at San José State University. Professor Bettelheim has traveled extensively, has done research throughout the Caribbean, and has visited West Africa tracing the continuities between African and Caribbean art forms.

MARGARET E. CRAHAN is a member of the Department of History at the Herbert H. Lehman College of the City University of New York. She has published several articles on Latin American colonial as well as modern history, and more recently has been working on two monographs dealing with religion and cultural dependency in Cuba during the twentieth century. Professor Crahan received a doctorate from Columbia University and has been the recipient of a number of major academic fellowships. From 1977 to 1980 she was the John Courtney Murray Fellow at the Woodstock Theological Center in Washington, D.C.

BARRY W. HIGMAN has a doctorate from the University of the West Indies, Mona, Jamaica, and is currently a member of the Department of History there. Dr. Higman is the author of several outstanding articles dealing with Caribbean history and demography, and his first book, *Slave Population and Economy in Jamaica, 1807-1834*, won the Bancroft prize in 1976. During the academic year 1976-1977, he was a fellow at the Shelby Cullom Davis Center, Princeton University. Dr. Higman has lectured at many universities in the United States, including Johns Hopkins, Rochester, and Harvard.

HARRY HOETINK is a member of the Center for Caribbean Studies in the Institute for Cultural Anthropology at the University of Utrecht. He has his doctorate from Leiden University and has twice served as the Director of the Center for Latin American Studies in Amsterdam. Professor Hoetink has taught at Yale University, the University of Texas at Austin, and the University of Puerto Rico, where he was the Director of the Institute of Caribbean Studies between 1969 and 1974. He is the author of *Caribbean Race Relations: A Study of Two Variants* (1971); *El Pueblo Dominicano* (1971); and *Slavery and Race Relations in the Americas* (1973).

FRANKLIN W. KNIGHT has been a member of the Department of History at The Johns Hopkins University since 1973. Prior to that he taught at the State University of New York at Stony Brook. He has a Ph.D. from the University of Wisconsin, Madison, and has written extensively on the Caribbean, as well as on Latin American and African themes pertaining to the Atlantic World. His books include *Slave Society in Cuba during the Nineteenth Century* (1970); *African Dimension of Latin American Societies* (1974); and *The Caribbean: The Genesis of a Fragmented Nationalism* (1978).

MAUREEN WARNER LEWIS is a member of the Department of English at the University of the West Indies, Mona, Jamaica. A sociolinguist by training, she has done research both in the English West Indies and in Nigeria, West Africa, and has published some of her findings in the *African Studies Association of the West Indies Bulletin*.

MONICA SCHULER teaches history at Wayne State University and has also taught at St. Mary's College, Notre Dame, Indiana. She has a Ph.D. from the University of Wisconsin, Madison, and has done research in Jamaica and Nigeria. She has published articles on Caribbean slave revolts and African migration to the West Indies. She has recently completed a social history of liberated African immigrants to Jamaica during the nineteenth century.

LORNA V. WILLIAMS is a member of the Department of Modern Foreign Languages at the University of Missouri, St. Louis. She has also taught at Indiana University, where she earned her doctorate, and at Dartmouth College. Professor Williams has published several articles in the field of Spanish American literary criticism, as well as a number of short stories. A collection of her short stories, *Jamaica Mento*, appeared in Trinidad in 1978. During the academic year, 1978-1979, she was a postdoctoral fellow in the Department of History at The Johns Hopkins University.

THE JOHNS HOPKINS UNIVERSITY PRESS

This book was set in IBM Selectric Press Roman by Culpeper Publishers. It was printed on 55 lb. Cream White Offset and bound by Publication Press Sales, Inc.

Library of Congress Cataloging in Publication Data

Main entry under title:

Africa and the Caribbean.

    (Johns Hopkins studies in Atlantic history and culture)
    Bibliography: pp. 146-57
    1. Caribbean area—Civilization—African influences—
Addresses, essays, lectures. 2. Caribbean area—
Religious life and customs—Addresses, essays, lectures.
3. Blacks—Caribbean area—Addresses, essays, lectures.
I. Crahan, Margaret E. II. Knight, Franklin W.
III. Series.
F2169.A37   972.9   78-20531
ISBN 0-8018-2186-X